Skelton's
Magnyfycence
and the
Cardinal Virtue Tradition

Skelton's Magnyfycence
and the Cardinal Virtue Tradition

By
William O. Harris

The University of
North Carolina Press · Chapel Hill

*Copyright © 1965 by
The University of North Carolina Press
Manufactured in the United States of America
Library of Congress Catalog Card Number 65-23139
Printed by The Seeman Printery, Durham, N.C.*

Preface

At the same time that John Skelton was writing his poetry, the morality drama of England was being eagerly written, staged, printed (and, in the process, altered) by that group of humanists we now refer to as the Sir Thomas More circle. Yet Skelton's connection with this dramatic activity is limited, as far as we know, to the fact that his surviving morality play, *Magnyfycence,* was printed by Rastell during the same busy years of the early 1530's when he was publishing his own and Heywood's theatrical pieces. Not surprisingly, then, A. W. Reed writes the definitive study of this group of pioneers in Tudor drama with only a passing reference to their contemporary, Skelton;[1] and Pearl Hogrefe's more recent study of the doctrinal ideas reflected in the plays associated with the More group takes cognizance of *Magnyfycence* only insofar as its thematic ideas seem to her to be in diametrical opposition to those of the humanists-playwrights.[2]

Our perspective of English dramatic activity at the opening of the sixteenth century, then, leads us to envision Skelton as something of an outsider in this age of dramatic

1. A. W. Reed, *Early Tudor Drama: Medwall, the Rastells, Heywood, and the More Circle* (London, 1926), p. 106.
2. Pearl Hogrefe, *The Sir Thomas More Circle: A Program of Ideas and Their Impact on Secular Drama* (Urbana, Ill., 1959), pp. 309-13, 346-47.

ferment, as a poet who happened to write a play rather than as a practicing dramatist knowledgeably immersed in the morality heritage, its limitations and potentialities. Medwall, Rastell, and Heywood we think of as dramatists (though they were also priest, printer, and poet); but Skelton we first think of as poet, not playwright. He is the angry satirist of Wolsey, the Hogarthian painter of alewives, the vituperative flyter, the creator of a saucy verseform, etc., etc.; and he also happened to write a play.

The poets of our own century who taught us to read Skelton reflect the view. Robert Graves exalts him, as "the dedicated poet," above Virgil; but his only concern with him as dramatist is to misquote the erroneous views of a character and allege them to be those of the playwright.[3] W. H. Auden is far more responsible, but he reflects a similar tendency when he says that "excluding *Magnificence*, Skelton's poetry falls naturally into four divisions. . . ." After the dismissal, he does return for a paragraph's comment, which begins: "Of Skelton's one excursion into dramatic form, *Magnificence,* not much need be said."[4] Among the scholars there prevails the same image of the poet who also wrote a play. There is a dutiful chapter on *Magnyfycence* in each of the six full-length studies of Skelton written

3. *Oxford Addresses on Poetry* (London, 1961), p. 7.
4. "John Skelton," *The Great Tudors,* ed., Katharine Garvin (1st ed.; London, 1935), pp. 59 and 67. It should be noticed, however, that Mr. Auden, who said of the play in this context that if "cut by at least two-thirds it might act very much better than one imagines," worked toward such a cutting a few years back when he and Noah Greenburg of the New York *Pro Musica Antiqua* started work on a production of *Magnyfycence;* unfortunately the production never came to fruition when financial backing failed to materialize. However, Robert Kinsman informs me of a successful production in England recently, further details of which he is citing in an article on *Magnyfycence* appearing soon.

since the poets revived him, but only in the last two have such chapters been more than perfunctory.[5]

It is both inevitable and, in many respects, just that the career of Skelton should so present itself to the modern student. For, after all, only *Magnyfycence* counterbalances all the poems; and what can the critic do but evaluate what exists? However, the danger lies in Auden's overstatement that *Magnyfycence* represents "Skelton's one excursion into dramatic form." Such is far from the case, though it is difficult for even the knowledgeable scholar to remain aware of it. Besides this surviving morality, Skelton himself claims to have written "Vertu . . . the souerayne enterlude," a comedy called *Achademios,* as well as an unspecified number of "paiauntis that were played in Ioyows Garde."[6] In addition, Thomas Warton gives a plot summary of a play, *The Nigramansir,* which he claims bears Skelton's name on the title page dated 1504.[7] Further still, W. W. Greg and

5. William Nelson treats the play only briefly in *John Skelton, Laureate* (New York, 1939), pp. 138-39. Separate but rather bland chapters are devoted to it in L. J. Lloyd, *John Skelton: A Sketch of His Life and Writings* (Oxford, 1938), pp. 76-98; Ian A. Gordon, *John Skelton, Poet Laureate* (Melbourne, 1943), pp. 135-46; H. L. R. Edwards, *Skelton: The Life and Times of an Early Tudor Poet* (London, 1949), pp. 168-77. Maurice Pollet's chapter in *John Skelton (c. 1460-1529), Contribution à l'Histoire de la Pré-renaissance Anglaise* ("Études Anglaises," IX [Paris, 1962]), pp. 105-27, goes beyond these by suggesting a striking analogue; but only A. R. Heiserman, in *Skelton and Satire* (Chicago, 1961), pp. 66-125, has developed an independent interpretation.

6. *Garlande of Laurell,* ll. 1177, 1184, and 1383 in Rev. Alexander Dyce, ed., *The Poetical Works of John Skelton* (London, 1843), I, 408, 409, and 416. John Bale, Skelton's near contemporary and biographer, classed the "paiauntis" as "theatrales ludos" but Dyce argues otherwise (II, 330-31).

7. *The History of English Poetry* (London, 1840), pp. 508-11. Identified by Warton as a morality but now apparently non-existent, the piece has long been doubted as a Warton fabrication (See Robert Lee Ramsay, ed., *Magnyfycence,* EETS, ES, XCVIII [London, 1908 (for 1906)], xviii-xix); however, Robert Kinsman has called my attention to the fact that Henry R. Plomer, "An Inventory of Wynkyn de Worde's House 'The Sun in Fleet Street' in 1553," *The Library,* 3rd ser., VI (1915), 233, observes that "part

Willy Bang would attribute *Godly Queene Hester* to Skelton,[8] as George Frost and Ray Nash would assign to him their discovery of the morality fragment, *Good Order*.[9] Even discounting some of these as unsurely founded, there remains sufficient evidence to view Skelton as one of those who, in the opening decades of the sixteenth century, knew through practice the dramatic heritage of the morality tradition and who worked creatively within its discipline. Though there is no evidence that he shared with the More group their endeavors to shape the morality heritage into a vehicle for humanistic thought, the extent of his playwriting suggests that he paralleled them in his interest in the morality play and its potentialities of form and theme.

An awareness of the possible extent of Skelton's work within the morality tradition certainly need not call for a re-evaluation of him as more dramatist than poet; but it should provide a context from which *Magnyfycence* might be most responsibly studied. As the work of a practicing dramatist who was as knowledgeably concerned with morality structures and themes as Medwall, Rastell or Redford, it should be approached with an initial assumption that, while its author might deliberately modify the inherited forms, he would not be likely to reflect a gross unconcern for or misunderstanding of them.

Robert Lee Ramsay's study of the play—by far the most influential upon modern scholarship—does not neglect the morality background; indeed, one of the most valuable

---

of the stock certainly came from John Raitell's [sic] printing-house, as the following items testify: . . . 12 copies of 'thenterlude of magnifycence,' and 100 copies of 'Necromantia,' the play of which no copy has been seen since the eighteenth century. . . ."

8. *A New Enterlude of Godly Queene Hester*, ed. W. W. Greg, Band V, *Materialien zur Kunde des älteren Englischen Dramas*, ed. Willy Bang (Louvain, 1904), p. XI. The ascription to Skelton is tentative at best.

9. "*Good Order*: A Morality Fragment," *SP*, XLI (1944), 485-88.

contributions of his introduction to the play derives from the detailed survey he makes of the morality patterns likely to have been inherited by Skelton.[10] Nothwithstanding, he assumes that Skelton's aim in *Magnyfycence* was "far from being the cultivation of the dramatic form for its own sake" (p. xiii), that instead the play is to be viewed as one of the Wolsey satires. These assumptions, as I suggest in the opening chapter of the present study, lead one to reject as organically irrelevant half of the morality structure because it contributes nothing to either this satiric purpose or the secular theme alleged to support it.

Thus, what we know of Skelton the poet tends to color what we can understand of Skelton the dramatist. But whereas, on the one hand, we are becoming more and more aware that the poet has a versatility far exceeding satiric monomania, such a study as David Bevington's[11] should make us more aware, on the other hand, that the dramatist knew his craft in a very thorough way.

The present study, then, assumes from the start the possibility that the play is the work of an artist well enough schooled in the dramaturgical demands of the morality tradition to have fully known what he was about in following the dual-conflict structure he adapts and in claiming for his play the kind of moral, if not theological, purpose characteristic of the early Tudor morality. Proceeding from such an assumption, the interpretation offered for the play is that it dramatizes not the usual virtue-vice struggle for man's soul but a struggle for a king's soul, conveyed in

10. Ramsay, ed., *Magnyfycence*, pp. cxxviii-cxcvii.
11. He demonstrates Skelton's artful mastery of so complex and practical a staging problem as that of the multiple-rôle divisions required to accommodate early Tudor plays to the four-men-and-a-boy troupes who performed them (*From "Mankind" to Marlowe: Growth of Structure in the Popular Drama of Tudor England* [Cambridge, Mass., 1962], pp. 132-36).

PREFACE

terms of the cardinal virtue considered appropriate to royal conduct, and that the struggle involves the full range of the morality structure. Skelton's modifications of the inherited genre are bold, but they are wrought in accordance with the structural-thematic principles he creatively respected.

My debts incurred while working with Skelton's play and its heritages have been many and are gratefully recalled. For assistance in publishing this book I am indebted to the Ford Foundation program of support for American university presses. Also, I would acknowledge with appreciation the University Research Committee of the University of Alabama for a summer's grant which enabled me to complete the manuscript. The libraries to whose staffs I owe thanks are numerous: the University of North Carolina Library; the Library of Congress; the Dumbarton Oaks Library; the Henry E. Huntington Library; and especially the Folger Shakespeare Library for two summer fellowships and for the most gracious and helpful staff any scholar is likely to encounter anywhere.

Of the many persons who have helped me in various ways, I would mention especially Dr. Ernest W. Talbert, to whom I am deeply grateful not only for his criticism and encouragement from the very beginning of this study until its fruition but also for what his teaching and his example in scholarly research have added to my understanding of the drama of Tudor England. To Robert S. Kinsman I would express my sincerest appreciation for his generosity in making available to me the wealth of information and insights he has garnered concerning *Magnyfycence*. Finally, as any husband knows, what he gains from his wife not just for typing, proofreading, and miscellaneous chores but for her orienting an entire family's existence to accommodate his research and writing habits is beyond computation.

Contents

Preface	v
1. The Interpretive Choice: Satire by Aristotelianism or Structural Integrity	3
2. Wolseyan Satire Re-Examined	12
3. The Meaning of "Magnificence" and Other Terms	46
4. Fortitude and the Two-Part Morality Structure	71
5. Three Interpretive Problems Solved	127
6. A Concluding Analogue	157
Index	169

Skelton's Magnyfycence
and the Cardinal Virtue Tradition

1 · The Interpretive Choice: Satire by Aristotelianism or Structural Integrity

It has not been recently fashionable to pay heed to John Skelton's strident protestations concerning the theme of *Magnyfycence,* his lone surviving morality. In the *Garlande of Laurell* he insists that "who pryntith it wele in mynde / Moche dowblenes of the worlde therin he may fynde."¹ Duplicity of Wolsey-like courtiers we profess to see in abundance; but it is Fortune, not fortune-seekers, about whom a virtuous character in the play says, "All her Delyte is set in Doublenesse" because

> Nowe she wyll laughe; forthwith she wyll frowne;
> Sodenly set vp and sodenly pluckyd downe;
> She dawnsyth varyaunce with mutabylyte,
> Nowe all in Welth, forthwith in Pouerte.²

The structural sweep of the play follows this cycle, from one temptation in wealth to another in poverty. Above all, it is in the epilogue that one hears the poet most insistently belabor the point, swelling to some fifty-five lines one mercilessly redundant refrain:

1. Ll. 1196-97. Citations from Skelton's works, except *Magnyfycence* and unless otherwise specified, are to *The Poetical Works of John Skelton,* ed. Rev. Alexander Dyce (2 vols.; London, 1843).

2. Ll. 2029, 2024-27. Citations from *Magnyfycence* are to Robert Lee Ramsay's edition, EETS, ES, XCVIII (London, 1908 [for 1906]).

> A myrrour incleryd is this interlude,
> This lyfe inconstant for to beholde and se:
> Sodenly auaunsyd, and sodenly subdude;
>   Sodenly Ryches, and sodenly Pouerte;
>   Sodenly Comfort, and sodenly Aduersyte;
>   Sodenly thus Fortune can bothe smyle and frowne,
>   Sodenly set vp, and sodenly cast down.
>
> Sodenly promotyd, and sodenly put backe;
>   Sodenly cherysshyd, and sodenly cast asyde;
>   Sodenly commendyd, and sodenly fynde a lacke;
>   Sodenly grauntyd . . .[3]

and so on and on. But we no longer listen.

Back even before the poet was given fresh voice by the Reverend Mr. Dyce, John Payne Collier listened, agreeing simply that "the moral purpose of *Magnyfycence* is to show the vanity of worldly grandeur."[4] So, too, A. W. Ward held that "*in construction and purpose* it has nothing to distinguish it from earlier moralities. Its object is, as one of the characters states at the close, to offer

> 'A playne example of worldly vaynglory,
> How in this world there is no sekernesse,
> But fallyble flatery enmyzed with bytternesse.' "[5]

Before such simple acceptance of the poet went suddenly out of fashion, Ward added another observation soon to become passé, maintaining that in *Magnyfycence*, "contrary to his practice in his Satires, Skelton abstains from any personal applications" (p. 129).

3. Ll. 2519-29.
4. *The History of English Dramatic Poetry to the Time of Shakespeare: and Annals of the Stage to the Restoration* (London, 1879), II, 242.
5. *A History of English Dramatic Literature to the Death of Queen Anne* (rev. ed.; London, 1899), I, 128-29.

These critics, naïvely repeating the poet's claims, were the last who in any way conceived of the drama as dealing with the world's doubleness as it dispenses "Sodenly Ryches, and sodenly Pouerte." E. S. Hooper reversed Ward's findings completely, maintaining that Skelton "abandoned the typical morality themes—the course of human life and the struggle of vice and virtue." Instead the struggle was seen to be that of "the opposition of moderation and prodigality," which was "appropriately chosen" in view of the personal satire embodied in the play—satire directed at Cardinal Wolsey *in the person of the protagonist, Magnyfycence himself*.[6] Until very recently, the new course thus set never changed substantially, Skelton's redundant protests notwithstanding. For, while Arthur Koelbing convincingly disproved this first effort to find personal satire as the play's *raison d'être,* he assented to the theme of prodigality, citing analogues to substantiate it.[7]

Both these studies were, however, merely forerunners to the detailed examination by R. L. Ramsay, which, because of the apparent strength of its proof, has until recently been accepted as definitive. Ramsay, too, ignores the thematic claims of the dramatist and, as a result, perceives a disparity between inherited structure and secularized theme:

> The form of Skelton's moral play is substantially the same as that of the *Castle of Perseverance,* written nearly a century before, and of almost every other moral play which is extant from that date to its own; but its theme is an absolutely novel one for the morality department.

6. "Skelton's 'Magnificence' and Cardinal Wolsey," *MLN*, XVI (1901), 213-15.
7. *Zur Charakteristik John Skelton's* (Stuttgart, 1904), pp. 150-52.

> For the first time, the morality was devoted to giving advice for this world instead of for the next; it was only a step till it should cease to give advice altogether. The theme of every morality that preceded *Magnificence* was the salvation of the soul, that of *Magnificence* is the preservation of worldly prosperity. The basis of the play, accordingly, is no longer a theological but a philosophical allegory (p. lxxi).

This philosophical allegory, introduced into the old morality framework much as new wine into old bottles, Ramsay argues to be based upon the concept of liberality found in Aristotle's *Nicomachean Ethics* (pp. xxxii-xliv, lxxii-lxxviii).

In addition, he reintroduces the theory of satire, which, like that of the Aristotelian theme, proves to be a deterrent to any view of the play's structure as organically conceived. Following the passage concerning the "absolutely novel" theme, he continues: "But the lesson of prudence for the prince is accompanied by a vast deal of satire directed at, if not to, the prince's court. *Magnificence* was not the first moral play to indulge in social satire, which forms the strength of *Hickscorner,* or even political satire, which is the impelling purpose of *Wisdom*; but it was the first to satirize the follies of the court, and the first to direct satire at particular parties and actual persons" (p. lxxi). Cardinal Wolsey is, of course, the "actual person" Ramsay advances as the major target of this personal, political satire he holds to be the play's "compelling practical purpose" (p. cvi). The Aristotelian theme exists as a means toward the more practical end of warning Henry against being gulled into bankruptcy by his all powerful minister. Since neither satire nor the theme of liberality is much to be found after the king's fall from power, "we may exclude altogether the fifth stage,[8] which is merely the conventional theological close" (p. cvii). For that matter, even less of the play need be considered germane to the issues since "stages IV and V are partly vague warning, partly merely the conventional *dénouement* of every moral play" (p. cxxv).

Until quite recently, contemporary scholarship has been thoroughly dominated by both satiric and thematic portions of this theory which truncates the play long before its conclusion. Ramsay's visions of Wolsey and of Tudor court intrigue not only won general acceptance[9] but stimulated the search for additional allusions[10] and even drew plaudits from a distinguished scholar as an outstanding example of the proper way to discover political references in Renaissance literature.[11] Uncritical acceptance of the theory persists to the present time, though reaction has begun to set in.[12] The Aristotelian theme posited for the play has won

8. While the play is printed continuously without scene divisions of any kind, Ramsay divides it into five major structural units, which he designates as "stages." I shall employ the same term.

9. E. N. S. Thompson, "The English Moral Plays," *Transactions of the Connecticut Academy of Arts and Sciences,* XIV (1908-10), 362; L. J. Lloyd, *John Skelton: A Sketch of his Life and Writings* (Oxford, 1938), pp. 82 ff.; William Nelson, *John Skelton, Laureate* (New York, 1939), pp. 138-39; Ian A. Gordon, *John Skelton, Poet Laureate* (Melbourne, 1943), pp. 137-38 and 144-45; H. L. R. Edwards, *Skelton: The Life and Times of an Early Tudor Poet* (London, 1949), pp. 170-77; A. P. Rossiter, *English Drama from Early Times to the Elizabethans: Its Background, Origins and Developments* (London, 1950), pp. 116-17; E. M. Forster, *Two Cheers for Democracy* (London, [1951]), p. 148; Irving Ribner, *The English History Play in the Age of Shakespeare* (Princeton, 1957), p. 36.

10. Madeleine Hope Dodds, "Early Political Plays," *The Library,* 3rd series, IV (1913), 393-95; and Paul Luzon Wiley, "Wolsey's Career in Renaissance English Literature" (Ph.D. dissertation, Stanford, 1943), pp. 140-43.

11. Edwin Greenlaw, *Studies in Spenser's Historical Allegory* ("Johns Hopkins Monographs in Literary History," II [Baltimore, (1932)]), pp. 59-70.

12. Most recently David M. Bevington subscribed to it in *From "Mankind" to Marlowe: Growth of Structure in the Popular Drama of Tudor*

equally widespread and consistent support, Heiserman's rejection of it and the present writer's brief foray being the only opinions to the contrary.[13]

It is the purpose of this renewed study of the play to suggest that, relieved from these two assumptions which have restricted our attention almost entirely to early stages, the play may once again be appreciated in the light of Skelton's own claims for it. This is not to say that a reader can or should return to the view of Collier and Ward that the primary purpose of the drama is to moralize upon the mutability of worldly vanity—though there is more to be granted this facet of the play than we have been wont to perceive. It is to say, however, that an interpretation of the play which validates the second conflict as well as the first and which shows the theme to be seriously concerned with the temptations of adversity as well as with those of prosperity will accord more with the dramatist's claims than does a reading that must ingore half of the "dowblenes" Skelton

---

England (Cambridge, Mass., 1962), p. 52, after A. R. Heiserman had challenged its validity in *Skelton and Satire* (Chicago, [1961]), p. 119, and the present writer had done so in "Wolsey and Skelton's *Magnyfycence:* A Re-Evaluation," *SP,* LVII (1960), pp. 99-122. The latter study, slightly modified, has been included in the present work as the following chapter.

13. Thompson, "English Moral Plays," *Transactions,* p. 383; C. R. Baskervill, *English Elements in Jonson's Early Comedy* ("Studies in English," No. 1, "University of Texas Humanistic Series," No. 12 [Austin, 1911]), p. 249; Greenlaw, *Studies,* p. 70; Willard Farnham, *The Medieval Heritage of Elizabethan Tragedy* (Berkeley, Calif., 1936), p. 217; Lloyd, *Skelton,* pp. 93-94; Nelson, *Skelton,* pp. 138-39; Edwards, *Skelton,* p. 173; and Rossiter, *English Drama,* p. 116, all readily accept the view. Heiserman exposes some of the serious weaknesses of such an interpretation while I have pointed out others and dealt with one in "The Thematic Importance of Skelton's Allusion to Horace in *Magnyfycence,*" *Studies in English Literature, 1500-1900,* III (1963), 9-18. The substance of my article reappears, somewhat altered, in Chapter IV of the present work.

insists may be found by anyone "who pryntith it wele in mynde."

Heiserman rejects the Wolsey and Aristotelian claims at least partly on the same ground as that advanced by the present study—that in accepting them "critics have failed to deal with the whole play."[14] However, his own view that the play is a satire upon "a syndrome of abstract political evils" and that Skelton devoted "his *whole* work to an attack on these evils—the abuse of common wealth by a weak monarch beset by flatterers" still does less than full justice to the last half of the play, ignoring as it must the second of the two conflicts about which the typical morality plot turns.

As Ramsay has shown in that extremely valuable analysis of the morality tradition which accompanies his interpretation of *Magnyfycence,* the archetypal plot for those morality plays of the "conflict" category is not as Heiserman calls it a "stock rise-fall-rise" (p. 68) or a "rise-and-fall" (p. 125) pattern but one which consists of two struggles or conflicts over the human protagonist, the first won by the vices, the second by the virtues. This is the pattern utilized by Skelton; there is a second conflict that must either be dismissed as irrelevant or shown to be organically related to the issues that dominate the play. As in *Mankynde,* this conflict takes the form of a temptation to suicide from which the hero is rescued by divine agents. Unless this struggle against despair in times of adversity can be shown to be thematically balanced against its counterpart (the struggle against immoderation and pride in prosperity), the play

14. Heiserman, *Skelton and Satire,* p. 125. Elsewhere, he argues convincingly that when the "satiric, Aristotelian allegory becomes 'theological,' after the downfall of the prince, satire becomes impossible, and the play falls apart," and he concludes, "We must deny the validity of distinctions which force analysis to obscure the formal unity of the play" (p. 120).

must be acknowledged an architectonic failure. If both conflicts can be shown to be relevant, then the poet's ignored claim that his play concerns "nowe well, nowe wo, nowe hy, nowe lawe degre; / Now ryche, now pore . . ." must be recognized as containing at least some truth.

It is the purpose of this study to show that, considered in tandem, both morality conflicts in *Magnyfycence* are structurally relevant in dramatizing a theme based upon the doctrine of the cardinal virtue of Fortitude (sometimes called Magnificence or Magnanimity) which required of a man—especially a ruler—that he resist by temperate action the temptations of both prosperity and adversity. This same ethical tradition, I would suggest, clarifies Skelton's subtly ambiguous use of the term "magnificence," accounts for some of the shorter dramatic motifs, makes meaningful the puzzling allusion to Horace rather than Aristotle as the authority for measure, reconciles the concluding advice *de contemptu mundi* with the more practical stress upon the preservation of earthly wealth, etc. Both the fact that so many of these enigmas of the play may be resolved by reference to this one ethical tradition and, most significantly, the fact that the full range of the play's action through both morality conflicts may be understood not as makeshift patchwork but as an organically conceived whole, consistent with the dramatist's repeated claims for it, make an interpretation in the light of this tradition far more satisfying than is the combination of satire and Aristotelianism, which has bypassed many of these problems and almost completely ignored the final half of the play.

Since, as suggested, the theories of Wolseyan satire and of Aristotelian liberality have so dominated critical approaches to *Magnyfycence* and still stand unchallenged and largely unexamined except for Heiserman's rejection of them, the present study will begin by a re-evaluation of the premises upon which these companion interpretations are built before turning to the tradition of the cardinal virtues and its relevance to the play. Thus, the following chapter and much of the next re-examine successively the questions of satire and of Aristotelianism.

2 · Wolseyan Satire Re-Examined

As a careful dramatic craftsman, Ben Jonson especially resented what he called "politic picklocking of the scene." Nor is it easy to blame him when one recalls how locks have been so picked by finding political personages and events concealed in Peele's *The Old Wive's Tale*, in *The Faerie Queene*, in *Macbeth* even. We might well listen with some caution, then, when it is said of *Magnyfycence* that "its adaptation of the traditional morality plot, its innovations in the traditional cast, its adoption of novel sources for theme and motives, its related method of characterization, are all mysteries to be unlocked by a single key,—its political application," which is held to be the play's "compelling practical purpose."[1] The approach is an ambitiously simple one—to explicate most of the phenomena of the play as serving one purpose, an attack upon Wolsey for his seduction of the king into prodigality against the circumspect advice of the conservatives at court under the Duke of Norfolk. Yet, while purporting to resolve all problems in the light of this one purpose, the interpretation creates an architectonic impasse: that half of the play which seems impervious to the theory of personal satire must be dismissed as mere verbiage. Before assuming so extraordinary

---

1. *Magnyfycence*, ed. Robert Lee Ramsay, EETS, ES, XCVIII (London, 1908 [for 1906]), cvi-cvii.

a conceptual failure or neglect on the dramatist's part, might it not be well to make sure whether the key has unlocked or the lock been picked? It is the purpose of this chapter to suggest that the latter is the case, that a reading of the play as an attack on Wolsey is insupportable in the face of (1) the chronological difficulties and (2) the evidence attested by the play, by the other works of Skelton, by the literary conventions that affected him, and by the primary historical documents of the era.

The question of chronology has seldom deterred the pursuers of Wolsey's image in the works of Skelton. Without much proof, he is alleged to have been a target in works written before he obtained his first benefice, or while he was still an obscure chaplain in France, or before he was in the Privy Council and Skelton had yet returned to court.[2] To read *Magnyfycence* as a satire against Wolsey calls for a similar disregard for probability.

While it is true that the Cardinal (by recent installation

2. Irving Ribner, "Morality Roots of the Tudor History Play," *Tulane Studies in English*, IV (1954), 24, cites *The Bowge of Court* (c. 1499) as an attack on Wolsey. A. F. Pollard, *Wolsey* (London, 1929), p. 101, hypothesizes that he was satirized in the lost *Nigramansir*, although Thomas Warton, *The History of English Poetry* (London, 1824), III, 185, says it was printed in 1504. F. M. Salter, "Skelton's *Speculum Principis*," *Speculum*, IX (1934), 29-30, says that Wolsey is "obviously" alluded to in the enigmatic words "Tolle Ismaelem, Tolle, tolle" that appear in the complaint appended to the *Speculum principis*, although the piece must have been written before 1512 (and possibly as early as 1509) and in spite of the fact that the poet castigated a known opponent under the guise of the same name (see H. L. R. Edwards, *Skelton: The Life and Times of an Early Tudor Poet* [London, 1949], p. 157). Since the first appearance of this chapter in *Studies in Philology*, LVII (1960), Maurice Pollet has also doubted the likelihood of any allusion to Wolsey in the Ishmael reference; he offers instead the suggestion that the allusion is probably to the king of France, whom Englishmen would have seen as "l'ennemi de l'orthodoxie, l'infidèle oppresseur" (*John Skelton* [*c. 1460-1529*], *Contribution à l'Histoire de la Pré-renaissance Anglaise* ["Études Anglaises," IX (Paris, 1962)], p. 84).

13

in 1515) had been a power at court for a few years, the peak of his ambitions, and the resulting concerted opposition, was not reached until some years later. Not until 1518 did he become papal legate *a latere,* and only after six more years of intrigue and political maneuvering was the appointment made on a lifetime basis.[3] It was this power, not the chancellorship, that engendered the opposition of both clergy and the old nobility (Skelton being a staunch defender of each). The contrast between episcopal acceptance of Wolsey at the time of the play and the opposition from the same quarter in later years is highlighted by Pollard's observation:

> The general cause for this particular hatred was, of course, the extensive supersession of episcopal authority by Wolsey's legatine powers.... The crushing effect of Wolsey's commissions, combining as they did the special jurisdiction of a legate *a latere* with the normal authority of an archbishop of York, provided a cause of resentment that was common to the archbishop of Canterbury and the bishops of both provinces. In 1515 bishop Fitzjames, in imploring Wolsey's assistance over the case of Richard Hunne, had protested that, if the cardinal could help the clergy in their weakness, they would be bound to him for ever. The legate *a latere* converted that devotion into an episcopal and clerical hostility which . . . promoted Wolsey's fall.[4]

Similarly, it was this power gained after 1518 which made potent the opposition of the conservative nobility under Norfolk. As will be shown later, at the time the play was written Norfolk and Wolsey were working in accord on the matters of highest national interest. Even as late as the fall of 1519, the Venetian ambassador reported that

3. Pollard, *Wolsey,* pp. 179-82.
4. *Ibid.,* p. 178.

the two were "very intimate."[5] Apparently it was the abuses of the legatine powers during the early 1520's which led to the open antagonism of the old nobility under the Howards. At least that is the implication of the third Duke's words when at last he removed the Great Seal from the fist of his enemy. Proclaiming his lifelong respect for Wolsey's titles (obtained by 1515), he frankly admitted his offense at the legate's political connections with Rome (secured in 1518).[6]

As a matter of fact, not only did the Howards base their opposition upon this power obtained years after the composition of *Magnyfycence* but there exists only the shakiest evidence that the poet was even associated with the family at this early a date. Before the *Garlande of Laurell* (1523), which speaks glowingly of the Countess of Surrey as his patroness, there exists no statement by Skelton, nor any solid evidence, of any connection with the Howard family. And the poet was never one to pass up opportunities to cite his connections with nobility. Only in his occasional poem, "Against the Scottes" (1513), and its Latin companion, "Chorus de Dis contra Scottos," does he even refer to the Howards. As Professor Nelson observes, one could hardly have celebrated the victory of Flodden Field without tribute to the brilliantly victorious English commander.[7] *Magnyfycence* cannot, on the basis of facts presently available, be considered a work commissioned by the Howards to attack Wolsey, as Ramsay implies.[8]

A *terminus ad quem* of 1516 not only weighs against the

5. *Four Years at the Court of Henry VIII*, ed. Rawdon Brown (London, 1854), II, 316.
6. George Cavendish, *The Life and Death of Cardinal Wolsey*, ed. Richard S. Sylvester, EETS, CCXLIII (London, 1959), p. 116; Pollard, *Wolsey*, p. 165.
7. William Nelson, *John Skelton, Laureate* (New York, 1930), p. 211.
8. Ramsay, ed., *Magnyfycence*, pp. cxxvi-cxxviii.

possibility of viewing the play in this light but puts any satire strangely at variance, chronologically, with the general vocal opposition to Wolsey and the flood of satires that soon accompanied this opposition. The wave of revulsion and protest that finally overwhelmed the Cardinal in the divorce proceedings had its inception no earlier than 1521. Wolsey's most reliable modern biographer dates the unpopularity from the Chancellor's taxation decrees in support of the 1521-23 war with France.[9] The execution of the popular Buckingham in the months just before this may also have been a contributing factor to the increasing discontent, especially among the nobility. Finally the disestablishment of monastic houses in 1524, which had actually begun in 1522,[10] aroused not only the clergy but the populace. Thus, the vocal opposition to Wolsey in England can be said to have begun and reached its sudden crescendo in the early years of the 1520's.

Consequently, it is not surprising that we find no extant literary satires directed against the Cardinal earlier than in these years of public discontent. Of the three surviving ballads satirizing him specifically, for instance, none can be dated before 1520. Both "An Impeachment of Wolsey" and "Of the Cardinall Wolse" contain allusions to the execution of Buckingham, and the former refers as well to the dissolution of the monasteries.[11] "The Complaynte of Northe to the Cardinall Wolsey" can probably be dated near the pardon on January 24, 1525, of Edward, later Baron North, after he had been imprisoned "for a book against

9. Pollard, *Wolsey*, p. 220.
10. Nelson, *John Skelton*, p. 189; Ian A. Gordon, *John Skelton, Poet Laureate* (Melbourne, 1943), pp. 151-52.
11. *Ballads on the Condition of England in Henry VIII's and Edward VI's Reigns*, ed. Frederick J. Furnivall, Vol. I: *Ballads from Manuscripts* (London, 1868), pp. 340-61, 331-35; see also Pollard, *Wolsey*, p. 225.

Wolsey."[12] That the growing discontent with Wolsey should find its earliest literary expression in the surreptitious ballad is not surprising; but that a morality play, the product of careful artistry, should antedate by half a decade or more not only these ballads but the public outcry that brought them forth is, to say the least, contrary to the normal expectation.

In addition to these three ballads, the book by Baron North, and Skelton's own satires, there exist half a dozen works that purportedly attack Wolsey; of them, *Godly Queene Hester* remains variously dated and seriously challenged[13] while all the rest are known to have appeared no earlier than the late 1520's. Roy and Barlowe's vigorous *Rede Me and Be Nott Wrothe* could not have been written before 1527;[14] Heywood's *Play of Love* accords best with 1528-29;[15] and Tyndale's two treatises, *Obedience of a Christian Man* and *The Practyce of Prelates,* appeared in 1527 and 1530 respectively. Much more relevant, finally, is John Roo's "goodly disguisyng" for Christmas at Gray's Inn, 1526. According to Hall's not unbiased account, the play

12. Pollard, *Wolsey,* p. 226. For the text of the ballad, see Furnivall, *Ballads,* pp. 336-39.
13. Though described on its title page as "newly made and imprinted this present yere, 1561," it was interpreted by W. W. Greg as a satire of Wolsey, dating between 1525 and 1529 (*A New Enterlude of "Godly Queene Hester,"* Band V, *Materialien zur Kunde des älteren Englischen Dramas,* ed. Willy Bang [Louvain, 1904], pp. VIII-X). However, such a view has been declined on various grounds by C. F. Tucker Brooke, *The Tudor Drama: A History of English National Drama to the Retirement of Shakespeare* (Boston, [1911]), pp. 131-32; A. P. Rossiter, *English Drama from Early Times to the Elizabethans: Its Background, Origins, and Developments* (London, 1950), p. 126; and Lily B. Campbell, *Divine Poetry and Drama in Sixteenth-Century England* (Cambridge, 1959), p. 209.
14. *English Reprints,* ed. Edward Arber (1868-71), XXVIII, 6.
15. R. J. Schoeck, "Satire of Wolsey in Heywood's 'Play of Love,'" *N&Q,* CXCVI (1951), 112-14.

was allegedly "compiled for the moste part . . . xx. yere past, and long before the Cardinall had any aucthoritie." Nevertheless, Wolsey

> imagined that the plaie had been diuised of hym, & in a greate furie sent for the said master Roo, and toke from hym his Coyfe, and sent hym to the Flete, & after he sent for the yong gentlemen, that plaied in the plaie, and them highly rebuked and thretened, & sent one of them called Thomas Moyle of Kent to the Flete, but by the meanes of frendes Master Roo and he wer deliuered at last. This plaie sore displeased the Cardinall, and yet it was neuer meante to hym as you haue harde, wherefore many wise men grudged to see hym take it so hartely; and euer the Cardinall saied that the Kyng was highly displeased with it, and spake nothyng of hymself.[16]

Far from suggesting an analogue to *Magnyfycence,* the statements by Hall serve rather to re-emphasize the unlikelihood of Skelton's having intended his play as an attack on the Cardinal. First, the date of Roo's play is enlightening. Like the ballads and other literary attacks, and unlike *Magnyfycence,* it appears in the years immediately subsequent to the national opposition to Wolsey. Secondly, this disparity between the dates of the two plays becomes even more suggestive when one observes that Hall uses as an apology for Roo the argument that the latter's play (like Skelton's) was actually written years earlier and hence could hardly be aimed at the Cardinal.[17] And finally, on the mere suspicion of satire directed at himself, Wolsey sent the

16. Edward Hall, *The Vnion of the Two Noble and Illustre Famelies of Lancastre & Yorke* . . . , [ed. Sir Henry Ellis, *et al.*] (London, 1809), p. 719.
17. For a different opinion, however, see Glynne Wickham, *Early English Stages, 1300 to 1600* (London, [1959]), I, 383.

author and a player "to the Flete." The same fate apparently befell North, and Skelton's satires brought such wrath upon his head that he was forced to flee to sanctuary. If, then, the satiric intent of *Magnyfycence* was so obvious that "to a spectator of 1516 . . . there could have been no doubt of the play's political application,"[18] how did Skelton's play escape the notice of the Cardinal? Could it not be that the play is not a satire at all, neither provoking the anger accompanying these productions nor bearing any proximity to them?

Of course, the immediate answer is that Skelton's personal opposition to Wolsey need not necessarily have coincided with the general antagonism and flood of invective that marked the 1520's. For, traditionally, the outstanding characteristic of the poet's career is considered to be that of lifelong, reckless, and implacable enmity toward the Cardinal. Ramsay, for instance, insists that "there is nothing in the facts, either of history or of the poet's life, that precludes the view that *Magnificence* in 1516 was his opening gun in a campaign" which ended only with the poet's death in sanctuary (p. cxii). However, since this assertion was made, just such facts have been uncovered which serve to make this view untenable. It is time these facts were brought to bear upon the problem of Wolseyan satire in the play.

For example, the heroic picture of Skelton unrepentantly resisting the might of the Cardinal even unto death in sanctuary has been demonstrated to be a myth.[19] First of all, the precise dating at 1527 of the poet's *Replycacion*[20]

18. Ramsay, ed., *Magnyfycence*, p. cviii.
19. For the original synthesis and a more detailed treatment of the matters touched on in this paragraph, see Nelson, *Skelton*, pp. 185-207, and his "Skelton's Quarrel with Wolsey," *PMLA*, LI (1936), 377-98.
20. James Bass Mullinger, *The University of Cambridge* (Cambridge, 1873), I, 605-8.

(dedicated to Wolsey) has destroyed the earlier assumption by Dyce (I, xliii-xliv) that similar dedications to the Cardinal appended to the *Garlande of Laurell* and *Howe the Douty Duke of Albany* (both 1523) must have been originally attached to earlier pieces and only assigned their present position through an error of Marshe, the first editor.[21] Now all three flattering appeals to Wolsey are accepted as having been written *after* the satires of the early '20's. Secondly, the tradition of the poet's death in sanctuary at Westminster has been shown to be the result of Bale's careless handling of his source. Thus, the poet's career seems no longer one of continued defiance even during declining years in sanctuary, but rather one in which Skelton's violent opposition in the early 1520's gives way, in the face of the Cardinal's reprisals, to abject flattery and efforts at reconciliation.

Regardless of whether Skelton continued to the death his open defiance, could it not be that *Magnyfycence* was in 1516 "the opening gun" in an extended campaign that was to include, in addition, the three famous satires, *Speke, Parrot; Colin Clout;* and *Why Come Ye Nat to Court?* Once again more recent scholarship needs to be brought to bear upon the problem. The chronology of Skelton's works arrived at by Fredrich Brie[22] and relied upon by Ramsay does indeed give the impression of a continuing series of attacks evenly spaced over a number of years. Supplemented by Ramsay's precise dating of the play itself, the chronology was as follows:

21. Ramsay's reliance upon this hypothesis by Dyce was implicitly self-contradictory, for the sequence of composition posited would have meant that the poet was writing poems flatteringly dedicated to Wolsey, during the same general period in which he composed the morality play that supposedly attacks him.

22. "Skelton-studien," *Englische Studien*, XXXVII (1907), 84-86.

Magnyfycence   1515-16
Colin Clout   1518-21
Speke, Parrot   1519-25
Why Come Ye Nat to Court?   1522

However, it is now known that a more accurate dating is as follows:[23]

Magnyfycence   1515-16
Speke, Parrot   late 1521
Colin Clout   1522
Why Come Ye Nat to Court?   autumn 1522

Not only were the three known satires written within the space of a year or so, but a minimum of five years separates them from *Magnyfycence*. When it is further considered that, within a year following the last of these satires, Skelton had been driven to sanctuary and was, with fulsome praise, dedicating the *Garlande of Laurell* (1523) to his tormentor, any theory of a lifelong attack on Wolsey (in which *Magnyfycence* was the "opening gun") becomes clearly untenable. Further suggestive is the date of the three satires in relation to the awakening general discontent with the Cardinal's policies. These were the very years of Buckingham's execution, the heavy taxations, and the closing of monastic houses. Skelton seems to have been not so much a forerunner in his attacks on Wolsey as the boldest spokesman for a generally outraged nation. And for his boldness he attracted the hostile attentions which the much earlier play apparently did not rouse. Thus the full chrono-

23. Nelson, *Skelton*, pp. 161-92. The process of establishing this chronology can be traced through the following articles: William Nelson, "Skelton's *Speak, Parrot*," and "Skelton's Quarrel with Wolsey," *PMLA*, LI (1936), 59-82 and 377-98; H. L. R. Edwards and William Nelson, "The Dating of Skelton's Later Poems," *PMLA*, LIII (1938), 601-22.

logical evidence would seem to weigh heavily against the view of *Magnyfycence* as a satire against Wolsey.

Nevertheless, conceding for the moment that, though hardly probable, there always remains the possibility that the play could have been an early attack, it might be well to study the arguments set forth by Ramsay. In undertaking to do so I shall adhere roughly to the two-phase approach by which he confronted the problem—that is, to study characterization as a clue to individual satiric portraits and then to turn to the plot of the play to discover if it is in any way a transcript of English political history for the years 1509-16.[24]

Concerning the first of these objectives, Ramsay advances the theory that the six vices of the play embody individually various traits of character which, when viewed collectively, convey a composite portrait of the Cardinal. This thesis is substantiated by extensively paralleling vice-speeches with known anti-Wolseyan passages from the later satires. The technique, a dubious one at best, becomes doubly suspect when one realizes that it is essentially the same used to "prove," just before Ramsay's work, that Magnyfycence himself was Wolsey.[25] Nevertheless, Ramsay bases the greater part of his thesis on just such evidence, which becomes increasingly unconvincing as one takes into consideration such factors as the conventions of Tudor moralities, the lifelong patterns of thought and expression of the poet, and even so basic a matter as the contexts from which paralleled passages are drawn.

For instance, personal satire is seen in the courtier-vice "Courtly Abusion, who is distinguished for the splendor

24. Ramsay, ed., *Magnyfycence*, pp. cx and cxx.
25. E. S. Hooper, "Skelton's 'Magnificence' and Cardinal Wolsey," *MLN*, XVI (1901), 213-15.

and extravagance of his dress; and in this we find another universal charge against Wolsey (cf. *Colin Clout*, ll. 310-22, *Speak Parrot*, ll. 451-3, 510, *Why Come etc.*, ll. 1136-43)."[26] Yet, if ever there was an object of general ridicule, it was just this foppishness of dress. From the period of Chaucer's Parson to that of Spenser's *Mother Hubberd's Tale* extravagance of dress was a subject of continual criticism. Indeed, within the narrower limits of the morality plays, no less than three other characters exhibit the folly of excessive dress—Pride in *Nature,* New Guise in *Mankynde,* and Curiosity in *Mary Magdalen*. And even Ramsay himself had noted that a passage from Barclay's *Ship of Fools* (1509) was so close in detail to the description of Courtly Abusion's exaggerated fashions as to suggest direct influence (p. lxxiii). To localize such a vital tradition of social satire into a specific allusion to Wolsey seems unjustified.

In a like manner, Ramsay interprets the vice Counterfet Countenance as a projection of Wolsey's ambitious striving for high place in spite of low birth. In support of the interpretation, Skelton's later sneers at the Cardinal as "suddenly upstarte from the dung-cart" and "cast out of a butchers stall" are paralleled with such lines from the play as the vice's charge that "A knaue wyll counterfet nowe a knyght / A lurdayne lyke a lorde to syght" (ll. 417-18) and another of his speeches that contains the passages: "A knokylbonyarde wyll counterfet a clarke," "A carter a courtyer," "A custrell," and "A counterfet courtyer with a knaues marke" (ll. 480-86).[27]

Again, however, a number of factors tend to make this parallel seem not quite so striking. First, the contexts of the

26. Ramsay, ed., *Magnyfycence*, p. cxiii.
27. *Ibid.*, pp. lxxxi and cxv-cxvi.

different statements vary significantly. The passages from the later satires are all portions of extended attacks upon some particular individual—clearly Wolsey. In contrast, the words of Counterfet Countenance are lifted from his monologue, a comic-moralistic self-analysis identical in form and purpose to those spoken by each of the other vices in this section of *Magnyfycence* and traditionally similar to countless such vice-speeches scattered throughout the English moralities.[28] Counterfet Countenance, like his fellows, devotes most of his speech to a catalogue of the various types of people who practice, in one way or another, his brand of viciousness. As he demonstrates, pretentious and dishonest concealments take a multitude of forms—from shams in the courtroom to hiding sand in sugar, from "counterfet maydenhode" to "counterfet Holynes." Only a small portion of the list is devoted to that particular brand of pretension which is characterized by the efforts of the low born to pass as members of a higher social order. And even this small portion is not aimed at any single person or type of person. The "tappyster" who would dissemble "lyke a lady bryght" rubs elbow with the knave who would "counterfet nowe a knyght." Thus, the intentions of the two types of passages are vastly different: the one is sharply personal; the other, broadly general. To extract from the latter a small, unrepresentative portion and claim for it the same personal intention evident in the former would seem a distortion, especially since upstarting in general was one of the favorite objects of social and moral criticism throughout medieval literature and well into the Elizabethan age.[29]

28. For example, the introductory speeches of Freewill in *Hyckescorner*, Wanton and Lust-and-Liking in *Mundus et infans*, or Pride in *Nature*.
29. John Peter, *Complaint and Satire in Early English Literature* (Oxford, 1956), pp. 96-98.

Even less substantial in Ramsay's proof is his statement that "Wolsey's low origin was the most common of all jibes used against him" (p. cxiii). That may be quite true, but in an age of unrestrained flyting such a charge was typical, whether based on fact or not.[30] Skelton himself must answer such a charge in his duel with Garnesche: "Dysparage ye myn auncetry? / Ye ar dysposyd for to ly" and counters with, "Thow claimist thé jentyll, thou art a curre" (Dyce, I, 128). Thus Skelton, the master of the indiscriminate invective, seems to have adopted this particular charge as a major weapon in his vast arsenal and to have used it on a wide assortment of opponents. For instance, much closer in wording and implication to the passage in *Magnyfycence* than any of those cited from Wolsey satires are these from an early lashing of an unknown opponent: "Lo, Jak wold be a jentylman," "An holy water clarke a ruler of lordys," "He braggyth of hys byrth, that borne was full bace," and "For Jak wold be a jentylman, that late was a grome."[31] Of course, the similarity in no way implies that the monologue in the play is aimed at this early antagonist; nor should *less* similarity suggest any relationship between the later satires and *Magnyfycence*. Adopted in his flyting, the charge of low birth and "up-starting" became for Skelton a favorite refrain, employed alike in squelching a rival, vivifying a passage of social satire, and attacking a chancellor.

If every charge of low birth in Skelton's poems were taken to be a possible reference to Wolsey just because the Cardinal was attacked on this score, the field of allusions

30. A. R. Heiserman shows, for example, that as early as the twelfth century the charge was a standard one and that it persisted to appear in the poetry of Dunbar as well as that of Skelton (*Skelton and Satire* [Chicago, (1961)], p. 285).
31. "Agaynste a Comely Coystrowne" (1495-96), ll. 14, 21, 24, 42. *The Poetical Works of John Skelton*, ed. Rev. Alexander Dyce (2 vols.; London, 1843), I, 15-16.

would rapidly expand to impossible proportions. Indeed, unlike the passages cited from *Magnyfycence,* many terms of low birth scattered throughout the poems are identical with charges made in the Wolsey satires. Take, for example, the *Colin Clout* phrase, "suddenly upstarte from a dung-cart," alleged to bear an affinity to the monologue by Counterfet Countenance, apparently because of similar expressions such as "a carter a courtyer." The precise charge was used by Skelton on at least two other occasions, neither of which could possibly have any connection with Wolsey. In answer to Garneshe's slur on the poet's own low birth, Skelton retorted in kind: "It cumys thé better for to dryue / A dong cart or a tumrelle" (Dyce, I, 129). And in a flyting piece written years before the Cardinal's rise, the poet had sneeringly proclaimed of an opponent that "Thys docter Deuyas commensyd in a cart."[32]

As a final example, "coistronus," as applied to the Chancellor in *Speke, Parrot* (l. 125), is the Latinized version of a word of contempt meaning, "a scullion, a kitchen-knave; hence a boy or lad of low birth, base-born fellow . . ." (*OED, s.v.* "custron"). The charge was a favorite one with Skelton, appearing in the title "Agaynste a Comely Coystrowne," in one of the poems attacking Garnesche (Dyce, I, 120), and even in *Howe the Douty Duke of Albany* (Dyce, II, 73), a poem dedicated to Wolsey. The danger of tracing repeated phrases in Skelton's works and arguing their exclusive application to a single individual is obvious. There is no end to it.

Yet a similar effort at identification by parallel passages

32. Dyce, ed., *Poetical Works,* I, 17. The puzzling allusion to "docter Deuyas" here, incidentally, was later applied also to Wolsey (*Colin Clout,* l. 1159). Skelton was in both cases falling back on a stock epithet denoting low birth (*OED, s.v.* "Deuce'"[1])—one which survived to be employed by a later master of invective, Thomas Nashe (see *ibid.,* II, 95).

is essayed by Ramsay with respect to a speech by Foly. The speech is a companion piece to the various monologues of the other vices and, like most of them, consists primarily of a catalogue of persons under his domination. Included are those "that come vp of nought," and who, having been "set in auctorite," then "waxyth so hy and prowde" that "all that he dothe muste be alowde." After confirmation by the other vices, Foly concludes with the assured conviction,

> For they that wyll so bysely smater,
> So helpe me God, man, euer at the length
> I make hym lese moche of theyr strength;
> For with Foly so do I them lede
> That Wyt he wantyth when he hath moste nede.
> (ll. 1258-62)

Reading the passage as intended for Wolsey, Ramsay not only lists parallels from the later satires but would view the concluding lines as an early version of what was later to be the famous "prophecy of Skelton" in *Colin Clout*, ll. 469-79 (p. cxii).

However, several objections to this type of reasoning are immediately apparent. Like that by Counterfet Countenance, the description by Foly is only part of a series, appearing between vignettes of folly-by-idleness and folly-by-tale-bearing, whereas the passages from the later satires are clearly focused personal taunts. Nor can Foly's concluding words any more be termed a "prophecy" than can the almost identical formulas to be found in the monologues delivered by his fellows. In fact, some of the others come much closer to suggesting a precise event, as, for example, that by Counterfet Countenance:

> Thus make I them wyth thryft to fyght;
> Thus at the laste I brynge hym ryght
> To Tyburne, where they hange on hyght.[33]

Furthermore, one must keep the allegory of the play in mind; it is Magnyfycence, the king, who is so led "with Foly . . . / That Wyt he wantyth when he hath moste nede." After the digressive social satire that characterizes Foly's speech as it does the monologues of his companions, the emphasis returns to highlight one of the central thematic concepts in the play, toward the dramatization of which the action is moving at that moment. Surely we push beyond the direct and obvious when we think we hear instead a prediction of Wolsey's fall some fifteen years in the future.

Most damaging of all to the proof by parallelism is the following passage:

> Promote a yeman, make hym a gentyl man,
> And make a Baylyf of a Butchers son,
> Make of a Squyer knyght, yet wyll they if they can
> Coueyt in theyr myndes hyer promosyon,
> And many in the worlde haue this condicion
> In hope of honour by treason to conspyre
> . . . .
> Such lokys so hye that they forget theyr fete
> On fortunes whele. whiche turneth as a ball
> They seke degrees for theyr small myght vnmete
> Theyr folysshe hertis and blynde se nat theyr fall.

The theme of the baseborn clambering for high estate, the reference to "a Butchers son," and even the prophecy qualify the passage much more strongly than Foly's speech as an allusion to Wolsey. Parallelism can achieve no surer results.

33. Ll. 421-23. See also ll. 742-44, 909-11, 1361-67.

Only, this passage is from the *Ship of Fools,* years before Wolsey's rise. The kinship to the lines from *Magnyfycence* is easily explained; Barclay's work is a known source for many of Skelton's vice-speeches, including this one.[34] Thus the play's lines in which, according to Ramsay, "Skelton probably comes nearest to dropping his veil of reserve" (p. cxii) actually show a stronger fidelity to inherited tradition than they do particularized kinship to the satires on Wolsey.

Similarly, reference to the poet's lifelong characteristics of expression and thought dispels the apparent parallelism between the vices, Fansy and Foly, on the one hand and comparable terms (and their synonyms) that appear in the known satires on the other. Passages such as the following from *Speke, Parrot* are advanced to support the identification:

Speke, Parotte, my swete byrde, and ye shall haue a date,
Of frantycknes and folysshnes whyche ys the grett state?

and the answer:

Frantiknes dothe rule and all thyng commaunde;
Wylfulnes and braynles no[w] rule all the raye;
Agayne ffrentike frenesy there dar no man sey nay,
For ffrantiknes, and wylfulnes, and braynles emsembyll
The nebbis of a lyon they make to trete and trembyll.[35]

However, too much emphasis is being placed upon Skelton's choice of terms in two different situations. While it is true

34. Ramsay, ed., *Magnyfycence,* p. lxxxi, notes this influence himself in another connection but neglects to quote the "prophecy" in Brant's work. The lines can be found in T. H. Jamieson's edition (Edinburgh, 1874), I, 187.

35. Ll. 410-11, 414-18 (Dyce, ed., *Poetical Works,* II, 20-21). Ramsay also parallels similar passages from *Why Come Ye Nat to Court?* (*Magnyfycence,* pp. cxiii-cxiv).

that the two fools in the play are called by an assortment of label-names, some of which are similar to those in the quoted passages, it is also true that Skelton had been bandying the identical terms around with monotonous repetition throughout his career.[36] But even more significant is the fact that the whole system of psychological, ethical, and political ideas conveyed by the terms underlies not the play and the satires alone but the whole career of Skelton. In one of his earliest poems, the elegy "Upon the Doulourus Dethe and Muche Lamentable Chaunce of the Most Honorable Erle of Northumberlande" (1489), he rebuked the disturbers of social order in the same terms he was to use in dramatizing the overthrow of a king and in satirizing an ambitious cardinal.

> What frantyk frensy fyll in your brayne?
> Where was your wit and reson ye should haue had?
> What wilful foly made yow to ryse agayne
>   Your naturall lord?[37]

Indeed, even earlier than this he had expressed his lifelong political philosophy: ". . . yf folye by his fantasie, disguysed with his gyrded habillementis of worldly vanyte, induce noble astates to daunce the comyn trace of abusion; wherupon, sone after, ensueth extreme confusion of fallyble fortune ful of deceyte."[38] Not only is the terminology iden-

---

36. See, for example, ll. 2 and 28 of "Agaynste a Comely Coystrowne" (1495-96); ll. 239-42 of "Ware the Hauke" (1504-12); l. 31 of "Agenst M. Garnesche Chalangar . . ."; ll. 118 and 148-49 of "Ageinst Lusty Garnyshe" (both dated 1513-14); and ll. 9-10 of "Against Venemous Tongues" (1516?) in Dyce, ed., *Poetical Works*, I, 15, 16, 163, 119, 130, 131, 134 respectively.

37. Ll. 51-54 (Dyce, ed., *Poetical Works*, I, 8). See also Nelson, *Skelton*, pp. 65-67.

38. John Skelton, trans. *Bibliotheca Historica*, by Diodorus Siculus, ed. F. M. Salter and H. L. R. Edwards, EETS, CCXXXIII (London,

tical to that supposedly reserved for Wolsey, but the whole passage might well serve as a summary of the first half of the play. The flaw in Ramsay's theory remains that it ignores the possibility—the probability—that the poet had, long before the advent of the Cardinal, a stereotyped abusive vocabulary as well as a strongly held concept of social order. The most logical explanation is that, confronted in his later years with a man incarnating the evils he had always opposed, he drew once again upon the same characteristic expressions he had used in his play and elsewhere.

Equally unconvincing is the proof that the other four vices were also later personified in the known Wolsey satires. From a passage in *Why Come Ye Nat to Court,* Ramsay calls attention to the following list of evils:

> Fals Flatery [Cou. Ab.?]
> Fals Trechery [Clo. Col.?]
> Fals Brybery [Cra. Con.?]
> Subtyle Sym Sly [Cou. Cou.?]

Even the personifying capitalizations and bracketed "equivalents" added by the editor (p. cxiv) fail to make the parallel convincing when it is considered that, not just vague equivalents, but the very names of the courtier-vices are to be found elsewhere in Skelton[39] and in other Tudor writings. The prologue of *Respublica* (1553), written years after Wolsey's death, states as the purpose of that play,

> To shewe that all Commen weales Ruin and decaye
> from tyme to tyme hath been, ys, and shalbe alwaie,
> whan Insolence, Flaterie, Opression,

1956), I, 359. The passage quoted is entirely an interpolation by the poet-translator.

39. See, for example, "Against Venemous Tongues" (Dyce, ed., *Poetical Works,* I, 134) and Salter and Edwards, eds., *Bibliotheca Historica,* I, 353.

and Avarice have the Rewle in theire possession.
But thoughe *these vices bycloked collusyon*
And by counterfaicte Names, hidden theire abusion
Do Reigne for a while to comon weales preiudice
pervertinge all right and all ordre of true Iustice
yet tyme trieth all and tyme bringeth truth to lyght
that wronge maye not ever still reigne in place of right.[40]

Similarly, Elyot, Tyndale, Grafton, and probably others used these terms as if they were popular catch phrases of the day.[41] Indeed, all four terms are much more likely to have been literary clichés than Skelton's exclusive terminology, especially reserved for use against Wolsey.

If the interpretation of *Magnyfycence* as a personal satire is to rest upon the evidence afforded by the paralleled passages examined in the preceding pages, it would seem to be validated by no strong proof whatsoever. Rather, the arguments become tenuous indeed when attention is given to the diverse contexts from which passages are drawn, when the poet's complete works are studied to determine if apparent parallels might not be characteristic modes of expression, and when attention is paid to vital traditions and other evidences of influence. And yet, except for further parallels from "other contemporary attacks on Wolsey,"[42] this is the extent of Ramsay's first division of his proof.

40. Edited by W. W. Greg, EETS, CCXXVI (London, 1952 [for 1946]), p. 2. Italics mine.
41. For Elyot's use of "crafty conveyance" see *The Boke Named the Gouernour*, ed. H. H. Croft (2 vols.; London, 1883), Bk. I, Chapter 26 (as cited in *OED*, *s.v.* "conveyance"); for Tyndale's see *Doctrinal Treatises and Introductions to Different Portions of Holy Scriptures*, ed. Rev. Henry Walter (Cambridge, 1848), pp. 128, 171, 221-22, 341; for Grafton's use of "cloaked collusion" see *OED*, *s.v.* "collusion."
42. In view of the evidence already cited as to the relative dating of the play (1516) and the known satires of Wolsey (1521-29), the three works mentioned by Ramsay fail to offer convincing proof. *Rede Me and*

There remains to be investigated, however, Ramsay's second contention that there is a "correspondence in plot, between the fictitious contest described in the play and the actual contest at court in the years from 1509 till 1516" (p. cxx). In so equating the conventional morality plot with contemporary events, he emphasizes primarily three factors, which I shall review in order.

First of all, on the basis of four references to France during the formation of the conspiracy group, a general allusion is thought to be made to Wolsey's having come into the king's service from France (pp. cxx-cxxi). However, the known facts of Wolsey's career tend to make improbable any recognition by a Tudor audience of such an allusion, while a close look at the relevant passages suggests an overemphasis on their significance. Concerning the first of these observations it is true that the young Wolsey, shortly after Magdalene College, served for a time as chaplain to Sir Richard Nanfan, an English functionary in Calais. However he did not enter the service of Henry VIII from this post. He did perform two minor diplomatic chores for Henry VII immediately following this early post in France, but upon the accession of the new king two years later, he received no post whatever. As a matter of fact, his name appeared (along with Skelton's) on the general pardon rolls. Not until the death of Henry's second almoner did Wolsey enter the service of the king in this mediocre position. Even then, in spite of a meteoric rise, he seems not to have attracted much notice before 1511, when he first en-

---

Be Nott Wrothe and *Godly Queene Hester* have been discussed. Polydore Vergil's allegations against Wolsey in his *Anglica Historia* do not appear at all in the MS probably written around 1513 but were interpolated at least as late as 1521, possibly as late as 1533 (see Denys Hay's introduction to his translation in the Camden Series, Vol. LXXIV [London, 1950], pp. xvi-xvii, xx).

tered Henry's council.⁴³ Indeed, Polydore Vergil's original manuscript contains no reference to his existence before 1513 (and then only in a single passage), and Hall's first allusion comes even a year later.⁴⁴ In view of these facts, any covert allusion to France in the expectation of suggesting Wolsey's sojourn there long before his service for Henry would have been hopelessly obscure to a contemporary audience. It seems hardly likely that four brief references to France should have suggested to a Tudor audience so early and so obscure a phase in Wolsey's career when the name of the hated foreign power carried so many other stronger connotations for them at the moment.

In this same connection, historical accuracy needs to be recovered with respect to the contention that Wolsey's early residence in France "was used by some to account for the pro-French policy that he always affected, whereas Norfolk sided throughout with German interests."⁴⁵ Apparently the only certifiable fact behind the statement is that Howard consistently supported an Imperial policy during this time.⁴⁶ As far as I have been able to determine, none of the contemporary records used by Ramsay, none of the significant modern historians of this period, and none of the literary satires of Wolsey relate his pre-1516 foreign policy to this early, indirect association with France. (Ramsay cites no authority for his statement.)

A similar lack of evidence marks the reference to "the pro-French policy that [Wolsey] always affected." Except

---

43. Pollard, *Wolsey*, pp. 13-15. Alfred Frederick Pollard, *Henry VIII* (2nd ed.; London, 1951), p. 44. John Sherren Brewer, *The Reign of Henry VIII, from His Accession to the Death of Wolsey*, ed. James Gairdner (London, 1884), I, 53n.

44. Hay, ed., *Anglica Historia*, pp. 208 and xxii; *The Vnion*, [ed., Ellis], p. 567.

45. Ramsay, ed., *Magnyfycence*, p. cxxi.

46. Brewer, *Reign*, I, 258n.

for his part in the diplomatic efforts to wed Princess Mary to Louis XII, Wolsey's actions up to this time could hardly have struck his contemporaries as "pro-French," for it was the appearance of the rising churchman in Henry's council in 1511 that marked the end of Henry's pacific attitude toward this country. Wolsey's agitation for an aggressive foreign policy led directly to war against France, in the managing of which he was the major figure. Indeed, it was from this vigorous *anti-French* campaign that Wolsey received, in 1514, his first rewards of power, stepping from almoner to the bishoprics of London and of Tournai (the latter recently captured in "his" war).[47] Furthermore, the affairs of 1515-16 served only to identify Wolsey more closely with anti-French sentiment. Polydore Vergil speaks of "Volsaei odium in Francum" as the true cause for the fiasco of the Milan expedition,[48] and surviving documents show conclusively that the recent Cardinal was most instrumental in the conduct of the affair.[49] One letter in particular is helpful in understanding not only Wolsey's position but the alignment of councillors in general during the crisis occurring at the time of the play. Dated July 17, 1516, it speaks of the opposition of Fox and Warham to the anti-French policy and reports that "the whole direction of affairs rests ... with the Right Reverend Cardinal, the Bp. of Durham and the illustrious Lord Treasurer [Norfolk]."[50]

47. Pollard, *Wolsey*, pp. 17-20; Pollard, *Henry VIII*, pp. 44-61.
48. Hay, ed., *Anglica Historia*, p. 234. The implicit contradiction in Ramsay's theory lies in the fact that he speaks at this point of Wolsey's pro-French bias and yet later emphasizes the Cardinal's strong hand in this anti-French campaign.
49. *Letters and Papers, Foreign and Domestic, of the Reign of Henry VIII*, ed. John Sherren Brewer (London, 1864-76), II, 1053-1136 *passim*. See also Brown, ed., *Court of Henry VIII*, I, 319-20; II, 12-16. For a more detailed examination of these events, see below, pp. 41-44.
50. Brewer, ed., *Letters and Papers*, II, 2183; Brown, ed., *Court of Henry VIII*, I, 252.

Actually, so well known was Wolsey's antipathy to the French that contemporary observers assumed it to be the basis for his having recently won the chancellorship and received a cardinal's hat.[51] In view of such unanimity of opinion concerning Wolsey's position, any references to France in *Magnyfycence* would hardly be taken as taunts at his supposed adherence to that enemy.

Like this external evidence from history, the internal evidence of the references themselves fails to support the theory. One reference (ll. 279-82) is to the demise of "largess" in France since the death of Louis XII (1515) and another (ll. 343-67) is a comic description of the hazards confronted by any traveler between France and England during the current period of hostility. Neither is a recognizable allusion to Wolsey's minor post in France. Superficially, a much more likely allusion would seem to be Counterfet Countenance's oath "by the armes of Calys" (l. 675), which Ramsay implies to be an oblique reference to the fact that it was in Calais that Wolsey held his brief post a decade previously (pp. cxxi-cxxii). However, once again one finds only that Skelton's penchant for stereotyped phrases is in evidence, for precisely the same oath occurs in *The Bowge of Court* long before Wolsey even went to France. Even if the name made any significant impact at all upon the Tudor mind, it would have been much more likely at that time to recall the massive English armies recently gathered there for the assaults on France[52] than to suggest Wolsey's

51. Mandell Creighton, *The History of the Papacy from the Great Schism to the Sack of Rome* (2nd ed.; London, 1897), V, 315; Pollard, *Wolsey*, p. 113. For evidence that this latter assumption had some basis in fact, see Brewer, ed., *Letters and Papers*, II, 780.

52. Brewer, *Reign*, I, 26-27. For an understanding of the focal importance of Calais in this connection, see the innumerable references to it throughout the first volume of the *Letters and Papers* in those dispatches relating to logistics of the operation.

insignificant and distant connection with the city. Finally, Ramsay says that "Courtly Abusion is also represented as coming from France" (p. cxx); but the relevant passage occurs in that vice's monologue where, satirizing lavishness of dress, he claims he introduced "This newe fonne iet / From out of Fraunce" (ll. 877-78). The point at issue is that "the newe gyse" comes from France. The distinction is a significant one, for, as Ramsay himself had earlier demonstrated, the model for his speech came from Barclay's *Ship of Fools* where the same popular charge was made that extravagance of dress "was brought out of France."[53] It is impossible to accept Ramsay's judgment that the four passages "can hardly be explained unless intended in some such way as a personal allusion" (p. cxxi).

The second of three supposed parallels between the play and the events of English politics during 1509-16 was suggested by two passages from Polydore Vergil, who claimed that Wolsey's early fortunes were pushed by Richard Fox, Bishop of Winchester, in order to counteract the power of Thomas Howard, then Earl of Surrey.[54] This allegation is equated by Ramsay with Fansy's intrusion through the forged letter from Cyrcumspeccyon (ll. 308 ff.), whose influence with the king he immediately begins to counteract. However, the ingenious paralleling collapses under the weight of the satire theory itself. For Cyrcumspeccyon is said to represent not Fox and his clerical party but Howard. For the episode to be in any way a recognizable allusion,

53. Ed. T. H. Jamieson (Edinburgh, 1874), I, 39. (See also Ramsay, ed., *Magnyfycence*, p. lxxxiii.) Evidence that blaming French influence for excesses in style may have been conventional at the time is suggested by such pieces as *A Treatyse of a Galaunt* (London, [1510]), in which also "rolled hodes stuffed with flocks," and "newe broched doublettes open at the brestes" are blamed upon the dandies "that out of Fraunce be fledde."

54. Hay, ed., *Anglica Historia*, pp. 152-53, 194-95.

the latter would have had to have been involved in Wolsey's entry into the king's council. Except for the simple allegory that, when a king is separated from his circumspection or clear reasoning, he is susceptible to the blandishments of his fantasy, the episode in *Magnyfycence* seems to have no further intent.

Finally Ramsay turns to that portion of the play in which the king relegates Measure into the control of Fansy and Lyberte and later, at the treacherous instigation of Cloked Colusyon and Courtly Abusyon, refuses his former counsellor's plea for reacceptance. Concerning these two "expulsions," the interpretation offered is that "precisely the same thing befel Norfolk (then Surrey) under Wolsey's instigation" (p. cxxiii). However, an examination of the historical evidence suggests something less than precision.

As to the first of these passages, Ramsay draws upon an obscure event in 1511. While Wolsey was still a lowly, if ambitious, almoner serving the aims of Fox, he wrote a letter to his superior, mentioning among other matters that Howard had gone to his home after an uncordial reception at court. However, the equating of this cryptic remark with the scene in which Magnyfycence [Henry?] deposes Measure [Norfolk?] at the urging of the vices [Wolsey?] offers a number of serious objections. First of all, the letter gives no hint at all of "Wolsey's instigation." The almoner is merely reporting one of a number of court incidents to his patron. That he approves of the turn of events is obvious from his opinion that Fox's influence might make Howard's departure permanent, "whereof in my poore juggement no lytyll good shuld insue."[55] But the very fact that he feels

---

55. Quotations from the letter are taken from Richard Fiddes, "Collections" in *The Life of Cardinal Wolsey* (London, 1724), pp. 8-9. The letter is merely summarized in *Letters and Papers, Foreign and Domestic,*

powerless without the aid of his patron indicates Wolsey's still minor position at court. Throughout the letter, the tone of subservience continues as he apologizes for any action he has taken (in other matters) without consulting Fox and expresses fear that his lord might be angry at his not having written earlier. But Wolsey's own awareness of his as yet subordinate and ineffectual position is most significantly conveyed by a passage toward the end of the letter, in which Wolsey mentions Howard again, "by whos wantone meanys his grace spendyth mych money and ys more dysposyd to ware than paxe. Yow'r presence shalbe very necessary to represse thys appetyte." Fox, not his aide, is the one who has the power at this point to influence the king and oppose a rival faction. There exists no evidence that Wolsey had a leading nobleman expelled from court in 1511.

Incidentally, the charge in the letter that the king's treasury is being exhausted through Howard's "wantone meanys" provides an interesting commentary on that nobleman's alleged leadership of a party committed to frugality in state finance. Actually, there seems to exist no evidence of his devotion to such principles during Henry's reign; rather, if one can accept the allegation in this letter, his inclination was in the opposite direction. This is the interpretation advanced by many historians, one of whom charges, for example, that Howard "knew how to conform himself to the humour of his new master; and no one was so forward in promoting that liberality, pleasure, and magnificence, which began to prevail under the young monarch. By

of the Reign of Henry VIII, ed. J. S. Brewer and R. H. Brodie (2nd ed.; London, 1920), I, 880 [3443]. Since volume I of *Letters and Papers* has been greatly expanded subsequent to Brewer's edition, I shall, when referring to this volume, cite the numbering in the revised edition and then, in brackets, that of the original compilation.

this policy, he ingratiated himself with Henry; he made advantage, as well as the other courtiers, of the lavish disposition of his master; and he engaged him in such a course of play and idleness, as rendered him negligent of affairs, and willing to entrust the government of the state entirely into the hands of his ministers."[56] One is tempted almost to cast Howard as the vice in the play, if it must be seen as a political satire. Certainly he seems an unlikely prospect for the opposite rôles of Measure and Cyrcumspeccyon.

But to return to the incident itself, the fact that the affair is unmentioned elsewhere in surviving documents tends to suggest that Howard's discomfiture, whatever its genesis, was a trivial one in contrast to Measure's continued neglect in the play. For Howard continued steadily to serve in extremely high capacities for the king. Less than six weeks after the letter in question, as England's Treasurer and Marshal, he was Henry's ambassador in drawing up the Anglo-Spanish league that was to determine the course of Englands' foreign policy for the succeeding years.[57] Soon after, he was made commander of the English forces at Flodden, where he won Henry's admiration and bestowal of the title, Duke of Norfolk. Taking into account these indications of continued service and preferment as well as the closer study made of the letter, one is not likely to notice any similarity between the morality episode and the events of 1511.

56. David Hume, *The History of England from the Invasion of Julius Caesar to the Revolution in 1688* (Philadelphia, 1828), II, 218 (Chapter XXVII under 1509). Both the *DNB* biography of Howard and Brewer's "Preface" to Brewer and Brodie, eds., *Letters and Papers*, I⁸, lv, substantiate this view, as does J. D. Mackie (*The Earlier Tudors, 1485-1558* in *The Oxford History of England*, ed. G. N. Clark [Oxford, 1952], p. 233), who says Howard "seems to have used his position as treasurer to promote a lavish expenditure."

57. Brewer, ed., *Letters and Papers*, I, 934, 935 [1980]. See also "Grants in November, 1511," no. 29, on p. 488.

In like manner, the second "expulsion" in the play fails to conform to any historical pattern. As a parallel to Measure's rejected efforts to regain the king's confidence, Ramsay suggests a passage from Polydore Vergil, which he interprets to mean that Fox, Warham, Norfolk, and Suffolk all retired from court in dissatisfaction with the projected military expedition to Milan in 1516.[58] However (1) Ramsay's use of the passages fails to reflect Polydore's true meaning, and (2) the statement by the historian is grossly inaccurate.

As regards the first of these, it should be noted that the passage has no connection whatever with the Milan expedition. Polydore concludes the statement with an assertion that "this was the sixth year from the start of Henry's reign and 1515 from the date of human salvation."[59] According to his recollection, then, the events must have taken place early in 1515, since Henry's sixth year of rule ended on April 21, 1515. Only subsequent to this passage does he discuss the Milan problem, stating that "not many days intervened" before Henry summoned a parliament and, having dismissed it, turned to the task of freeing Tournai completely from French connections. This in turn, according to the historian, led to the Milan proposal concerning which he says "William [Warham] archbishop of Canterbury, Richard [Fox] bishop of Winchester, Thomas duke of Norfolk, Sir Thomas Lovell and many others were accordingly summoned a few days later and opinions were expressed concerning the manner in which the affair should be handled."[60]

58. Hay, ed., *Anglica Historia*, pp. 230-33. See Ramsay, ed., *Magnyfycence*, pp. cxxiii-cxxiv.
59. Hay, ed., *Anglica Historia*, pp. 232-33. [Atque hic annus sextus Henrico a gubernatione regni fuit, et ab humana salute MDXV.]
60. *Ibid.*, pp. 234-35. [Perinde paucis post diebus Gulielmo Cantauriensi, Ricardo Vintoniensi episcopis, Thoma Northfolchiae duce, Thoma Louello equite, ac plerisque aliis accitis, de negotio gerendo sententiae dicuntur.]

41

Thus what Polydore actually says about Norfolk and the Milan expedition is that he was consulted, along with the highest advisors in the land.

In addition to Ramsay's misleading use of Polydore's words, there is the unreliability of the historian in this particular passage. For example, the resignations of Fox and Warham are said to have come before April 21, 1515; and the parliament, to have come after this date and been dismissed before the Milan diversion was initiated. In this year, Henry's third parliament met in two sessions, only one of which was summoned after the date in question. The first session met between February 5 and April 5; the second convened on November 12 and was dismissed on December 22.[61] Thus, if one accepts Polydore's record as accurate (as Ramsay apparently does), the parliament to which he refers must have been the second session. However, the negotiations for the subsidizing of Maximilian occurred long before this session began.[62] Furthermore, the account of the two resignations is garbled since Warham's retirement came, not before either session but two days after the dismissal of the second, and Fox's not until the next spring.[63]

Of course, these errors are minor ones, mentioned here only for the sake of indicating the caution needed in using an account compiled some fifteen years after the events discussed. Of a much more serious nature is Polydore's inaccuracy regarding the position of Howard in these affairs. Whether explained as misrepresentation or as an error, the fact is that his history contains the only suggestion that

61. *Journal of the House of Lords* ([London], n.d.), I, 18-56. See also Brewer, ed., *Letters and Papers,* II, 119 and 1130.
62. Brewer, ed., *Letters and Papers,* II, 1053-1154 *passim.*
63. *Ibid.,* 1335, 1386, and 1814.

the Duke of Norfolk retired in frustration at this time—or, as Ramsay would have it, that he was expelled. On the contrary there is abundant evidence that he played a major rôle in the war effort (which, of course, he would logically have approved, all other things being equal). A clearer perspective can be gained only by access to more authentic, contemporary accounts.

It has been suggested that, if Polydore did not deliberately invent Norfolk's supposed resignation, he may have confused him with the younger Howard.[64] The possibility is logical in view of the historian's late composition from earlier jottings; for during the period of the Milan undertaking, young Surrey and several other lords were expelled from the council because of their extravagant maintenance of men in livery.[65] Or the explanation may lie in the fact that Norfolk was, for a time during this year, extremely ill and thus away from court.[66]

Whatever the explanation, Polydore's statement is entirely fallacious. Norfolk's authority at court was very great and his active support of the expedition repeatedly attested. The Venetian ambassador, in his confidential reports, speaks of him during this crisis as "a person of authority" and as "one of those who manages these present matters." Indeed, the very letter to which Ramsay alludes as mentioning those who left court in opposition to the war shows not that Howard was among these but that " 'the whole direction of affairs rests . . . with the Right Reverend Cardinal,

---

64. Edwards, *Skelton*, p. 281.
65. Brewer, ed., *Letters and Papers*, II, 1959, 2018; Pollard, *Wolsey*, p. 76. The episode, incidentally, further destroys any picture of the Howards as the symbol of moderation persecuted by the forces of prodigality.
66. Brewer, ed., *Letters and Papers*, II, 1959, 2470. For a full transcription of the latter item, see Brown, ed., *Court of Henry VIII*, I, 309-12.

43

the Bp. of Durham and the illustrious Lord Treasurer [Norfolk].' "[67] These evaluations by Giustinian are borne out by the fact that, as early as July 6, 1515, and continuing until well after the Treaty of Noyons (the *terminus ad quem* assigned by Ramsay), it was Norfolk along with Wolsey with whom the ambassador dealt regarding the hostilities. During the same time Howard and Wolsey alone received the secret dispatches from English agents dealing with Maximilian; Howard was always in the small circle of advisors with whom the king conferred on the project; and (with Wolsey and the Bishop of Durham) he worked out and signed the league with the Pope, the Emperor, Spain, and the Swiss against France.[68] Such activities do not suggest expulsion from court. Apparently, Howard had a strong hand in the very affairs alleged to represent "the most crushing defeat of the party of Norfolk and the crowning triumph of Wolsey." Consequently, it is difficult to imagine that a Tudor audience, even one informed of the intricacies of court struggles and foreign intrigue, could have recognized in the scene of Fansy's rise and of Measure's futile and betrayed efforts to regain his place at court any parallels to "precisely the same thing [befalling Howard] under Wolsey's instigation."

With regard to none of the three alleged parallels does the evidence of historical records provide, then, any basis for assuming the plot to correspond to "the actual contest at

67. Brown, ed., *Court of Henry VIII*, I, 138, 309; Brewer, ed., *Letters and Papers*, II, 2183.
68. Brown, ed., *Court of Henry VIII*, I, 108-10, 138-40, 148-51, 160-62, 309-12; Brewer, ed., *Letters and Papers*, II, 2712 and 2231-32; Brown, ed., *Court of Henry VIII*, I, 168 and 307. Brewer, ed., *Letters and Papers*, II, 2462, 2486. Howard's position at court is further evidenced by his attendance at Star Chamber hearings (*ibid.*, II, 1856) and his and his wife's important rôles (alongside Wolsey) at the christening of Henry's daughter that year (*ibid.*, 1585).

court in the years from 1509 until 1516." Even more indicative of the pitfalls of such a theory of transcribed history and personal satire are the conclusions deduced from what events *do not* find their way into the play. Noting rapidly some of the events in Henry's and in Wolsey's careers subsequent to the date assigned the play, Ramsay points out that "these events find no place in the allegory of the play. Nor did any marked Adversity befall Henry under the direction of Wolsey. . . . Neither do we find any repentance on the part of the monarch or recall of his earlier councillors" (p. cxxv). This failure to find any correlation between history and plot in the final two stages of the play leads to two conclusions: (1) that the dating of the play in 1516 is confirmed, and (2) that the play can be neatly cloven between the earlier, relevant scenes of "veiled narrative" and the later, easily dispensable scenes, which represent "merely the conventional *dénouement* of every moral play." While the first of these conclusions merely borders on some dubious circular reasoning,[69] it is the second that has led to our twentieth-century acceptance of *Magnyfycence* as only half a play. However, if, as our closer scrutiny of the evidence would suggest, there is little or no basis for assuming any personal satire as the primary intent of the play, there need be no assumption that the play is structurally disunified. Of incidental social satire there is plenty, in both opening and closing halves; but of direct personal satire as the major formative principle that shapes only part of the morality before it drifts into purposelessness there is very little evidence.

69. At the outset, Ramsay predicates his theory of satire on his dating of the play around 1515-16 (p. cvii) and concludes, in reverse, by offering as confirmation of that date the fact that he finds no allusions in the play to events after this time.

3 · The Meaning of "Magnificence" and Other Terms

The twentieth-century approach to *Magnyfycence* which negates any view of it as an architectonically conceived whole, which instead regretfully apologizes for the last half of the play as irrelevant, is based not only upon the assumption that Wolseyan satire in the opening stages represents the "compelling practical purpose" of the drama but upon a companion assumption that the ethical ideas dramatized in the play are distinctly Aristotelian, the theme being one patterned on the concept of "magnificence" (or is it "liberality"?) found in the *Nicomachean Ethics* and its medieval derivatives. Since this "absolutely novel theme" for a morality Ramsay finds evident primarily in the early stages of the play, he dismisses the later portions as "merely the conventional theological close," an atrophied remnant of the old form.

As previously noted, A. R. Heiserman's recent study, like the present one but entirely independent of it, has challenged the validity of this interpretation, coming to the conclusion that "Skelton need not have read Aristotle in order to employ the term or concept of magnificence in his interlude" (p. 77). Such is the contention of the present chapter as well. However, it must be noted that agreement in dismissing the Aristotelian interpretation does not imply agreement between us as to the source of Skelton's ideas or the theme of the play. The nature and extent of our agreements and disagreements will, it is hoped, become apparent in this and the following chapter, which will deal with the thematic ideas of the play: their sources and traditional backgrounds and their relationship to the morality structure.

"The extent to which novel material has been injected into the old morality fabric," asserts Ramsay, "can best be gauged through the characters" (p. lxxii), some few of whom, appearing in the latter scenes of the play, are mere survivals of the morality tradition, but most of whom are given a secular emphasis derived largely from the *Nicomachean Ethics* (p. xxxii). The contradictions implicit in so sharp a division between conventional and radical concepts become apparent when, for instance, Dyspare is said to be "taken from the traditional morality cast without being wrought into adequate connection with the new allegory" but also is included among the "really new allegorical conceptions, which replace and not merely rename older figures" (pp. xxx and xxxii), or when the terms Foly and Largess are said at one point to be derived ultimately from Aristotle (p. xxxii), though the former is at the same time grouped among the "older morality names" and the latter is admitted to be "hardly an Aristotelian term" (p. xl).

But these are mere inconsistencies, indicative mostly of the pitfalls awaiting any classification that is too doctrinaire. More significant because of its positive affirmation is Ramsay's major statement concerning terminology: "Magnificence, Measure, Felicity, are distinctively Aristotelian terms; and the same origin, less immediate, is discernible for Circumspection and Liberty, Fancy and Largess, Folly and Conceit" (p. xxxii). Because of its centrality to the Aristotelian interpretation being advanced, the statement demands closer study. The opening assertion concerning Magnyfycence itself is, of course, the true crux of the problem; but before considering it I would examine the less central claim as to Cyrcumspeccyon, Lyberte, and Fansy.

Representing as they do behind the façade of Skelton's label-names simply the traditional concepts of Reason and Will, Cyrcumspeccyon and Lyberte dramatize in his play the lifelong creed manifest throughout Skelton's poetry. For he, as one critic expressed it, "conceived that the essence of morality, both personal and political, was to be found in the relationship obtaining between will (freedom of action) and wit (reason)."[1] As noticed in the preceding chapter, Skelton, in one of his earliest poems, chides those who disturbed the order of society: "Where was your wit and reson ye should haue had? / . . . / Ye armyd you with will, and left your wit behynd."[2] Years later, long after *Magnyfycence,* he continues in the same way to express his conservative dismay at the world "nowadays":

> For wyll dothe rule all thynge,
> Wyll, wyll, wyll, wyll, wyll,
> He ruleth alway styll.
> Good reason and good skyll,
> They may garlycke pyll.[3]

On another occasion he says it again:

> But reason and wyt wantyth theyr prouyncyall
> When wylfulnes is vycar generall,

---

1. William Nelson, *John Skelton, Laureate* (New York, 1939), p. 66.
2. "Upon the Doulourus Dethe and Muche Lamentable Chaunce of the Most Honorable Erle of Northumberlande," ll. 52 and 55 (*The Poetical Works of John Skelton,* ed. Rev. Alexander Dyce [2 vols.; London, 1843], I, 8).
3. *Why Come Ye Nat to Court?* ll. 102-6 (*ibid.,* II, 30).

and complains that "so ys all thyng wrowghte wylfully withowte reson and skylle."[4] His morality play opens with the same views, expressed in the same language. The very opening line proclaims the ideal, "Al thyng ys contryuyd by mannys Reason," but soon it must be acknowledged sorrowfully that "Wyll hath Reason so vnder subieccyon, / And so dysordereth this worlde ouer all / That Welthe and Felicitie is passynge small" (ll. 19-21). This thematic motif treating the hierarchical relationship between reason and will, and the loss of order when the hierarchy is violated, is no more consciously part of an Aristotelian complex of ideas in the play than it is in Skelton's other poetry, where it appears with such regularity.

Indeed, had these commonplaces not found their way into his writing there might have been more cause for attention. For, as has been so often and so fully demonstrated[5] as to require no detailed re-examination here, the psychological presuppositions embodying this reason-will relationship permeated the culture of medieval and renaissance Europe, finding important literary expression even as late as *Paradise Lost*. To cite such passages in the literature of Skelton's age would, of course, carry us far too digressively afield. Only one need be quoted to be representative for all the rest: "But if manne do forgette to set Wyll under the governaunce of rayson, and with a circumspect deliberation, to appoint unto hir limites and bondes . . . forth with the senses do prepare themselfes eftsones to

4. *Speke, Parrot*, ll. 55-56, 48 (*ibid.*, II, 4 and 24).
5. See, for example, Joseph Coleman Green, *The Medieval Morality of "Wisdom, Who Is Christ"*: *A Study in Origins* (Nashville, Tenn., 1938), pp. 48-55; Ruth Leila Anderson, *Elizabethan Psychology and Shakespeare's Plays* ("University of Iowa Humanistic Studies," III [Iowa City, 1927]), pp. 7-28; Lily B. Campbell, *Shakespeare's Tragic Heroes, Slaves of Passion* (New York, 1952), pp. 63-72, 93-102.

rebell. And affectes . . . do prepare them with wanton countenaunce and pleasaunt promyses to allure eftesones Will to their appetite."[6]

So, quite conventionally, when the action of *Magnyfycence* begins with Lyberte complaining that he "hath ben lockyd vp and kept in the mew," he is reminded that "Lyberte may somtyme be to large, / But yf Reason be regent and ruler of your barge" (ll. 35-38). Though the king begins by so subordinating his "will," he is soon approached by Fansy, who, claiming recommendation from Cyrcumspeccyon, perverts this resolve, frees the will from constraint, and makes way for those vices which come with their "wanton countenaunces and pleasaunt promyses."

At this juncture, it would be well to consider briefly the allegory implicit in Fansy, who comes claiming to be "reason's" envoy. Ramsay, of course, advances an Aristotelian equivalent—incontinence (*Ethics,* IV, vi). But the analogy seems needlessly drawn from afar, since the very same psychological system that clarifies Lyberte and Cyrcumspeccyon also has its "fantasy," which corresponds closely to the character in Skelton's play. The fantasy is that faculty, inferior to both reason and will, which is responsible for translating sense perception into thought and transmitting it to the reason for its ultimate judgment and to the will for its volition in the light of reason's judgment. Unsoundness of the organ of fantasy, no less than perversity of the will, can be a cause which "does not permit reason to hold the supremacy which it deserves."[7] According to the *OED,* as the preference in spelling shifted from "fantasy" to "fancy," the word came to designate also the mental

6. Sir Thomas Elyot, *Of the Knowledg which Maketh a Wise Man. A disputacion Platonike* (London, 1533), *Palestra,* LXXXIII (1920), 61, as cited in Anderson, *Elizabethan Psychology,* p. 139.

7. Anderson, *Elizabethan Psychology,* pp. 14-24 *passim.*

impression itself until, by Skelton's age, it had taken a further pejorative step to mean "delusive imagination . . . the fact or habit of deluding oneself into imaginary perceptions."

In this light, one understands the character of Fansy within the play, who deludes with false appearances, whose letter shunts reason (Cyrcumspeccyon) aside, whose deception eventually looses the restive will (Lyberte) from its proper restraint. The hierarchical disorder is complete when Magnyfycence, in the absence of Cyrcumspeccyon, turns his prosperity over to the inferior faculties, Lyberte and Fansy. Admonitions that "It is good yet that Lyberte be ruled by Reason" (l. 1387) are now rebuffed while a sycophant's flattery, "All that ye say, Syr, is Reason and Skyll" (l. 1381), goes undetected in its sophistry. Another boldly advises the now licentious king:

> By waywarde Wylfulnes let eche thynge be conuayed;
> What so euer ye do, folowe your owne Wyll;
> Be it Reason or none, it shall not gretely skyll.
>
> (ll. 1594-96)

Fidelity to the popular psychology of the age continues apparent as the king abandons himself to his sensual appetites and next subordinates even his fantasy and his will to the control of Pleasure (Courtly Abusyon) and others, who promise "to do you seruyce after your Appetyte" (l. 1793). The appetites of sense, residing in the vegetal soul, have usurped control even from the perverted will and a defective fantasy, who had supplanted reason. As Milton expresses it:

> For Understanding rul'd not, and the Will
> Heard not her lore, both in subjection now

> To sensual Appetite, who from beneathe
> Usurping over sovran Reason claimd
> Superior sway.[8]

Skelton's conventionality—or, rather, his dramaturgical embodiment of conventional psychology—may possibly even be seen in the episode of Fansy's terrified announcement of the disaster that the final usurpation has brought about. Skelton depicts Fansy as uncontrollably distraught by the sense of impending doom that is upon him as well as the king. Similarly, one student of the psychology of the age observes that the "faculty by which fancy is begot is more likely . . . to follow sense than reason; with satiation of sense fancy therefore dies."[9]

During his suffering, Magnyfycence is repeatedly made aware of his psychological error. When he exclaims, "What! hath Sadnesse [Reason] begyled me so?" Fansy responds, "Nay, maddnesse hath begyled you and many mo; / For Lyberte is gone, and also Felycyte" (ll. 1855-57). He is urged by Pouerte to "Put your Wyll to His wyll" (l. 1997), and Lyberte himself comes, proclaiming, "I am a vertue yf I be well vsed, / And I am a vyce where I am abused" (ll. 2101-2).

The rescue from adversity brings the return of the long-absent Cyrcumspeccyon, who chides that reason "inhateth all rennynge astray. / But, Syr, by me to rule fyrst ye began." Magnyfycence confesses, "My Wylfulnesse, Syr, excuse I ne can" (ll. 2430-32), and the fraud of Fansy is uncovered. Finally, Cyrcumspeccyon contributes to the king's re-edification the reminder that "Lyberte to a lorde be-

---

8. *Paradise Lost*, ix, 1127-31. *The Works of John Milton*, II² (New York, 1931), 300.
9. Anderson, *Elizabethan Psychology*, p. 27.

longyth of ryght, / But wylfull Waywardnesse muste walke out of the way" (ll. 2485-86).

This whole pattern of psychological concepts woven into the larger fabric of the play[10] is thus consistent not only with the poet's lifetime refrain but with the popular theories of the age. Nor are these conventional truths foreign to the tradition of the morality play itself. The tedious instruction of Man which opens *Nature* (and sets its heavy-handed tone ever after) stresses above all else these principles of scholastic psychology. Before anyone else can speak, Nature herself delivers a ponderously long sermon of edification to Man, climaxing it all by giving him "Reason to govern thee in thy way, / And Sensuality upon thine other side. / But Reason I depute to be thy chief guide."[11] Man is duly impressed and appreciative of this rational power,

> whereby I may aview
> And well discern what is to be done;
> Yet, for all that, have I free election
> [To] do what I will, be it evil or well.
>
> (p. 47)

But Nature must make the point one more time:

> Let Reason thee govern in every condition,
> For, if thou do not to his rule incline,
> It will be to thy great mischief and ruin.

10. The summary from the play in the preceding paragraphs is intended not as a digest of the full play but merely as a summary of those scenes that make up the psychological allegory, which is only part of a larger allegory.

11. *Recently Recovered "Lost" Tudor Plays, with Some Others*, ed. John Stephens Farmer (London, 1907), p. 46. In view of the rôle of Reason indicated by this and the following passages, it is difficult to accept Ramsay's assertion that Reason was "a neutral figure . . . in earlier moralities" (*Magnyfycence*, ed. Robert Lee Ramsay, EETS, ES, XCVIII [London, 1908 (for 1906)], xxxv).

> I wot well Sensuality is to thee natural,
> And granted to thee in thy first creation.
> But, notwithstanding, it ought to be over all
> Subdued to Reason, and under his tuition.
> Thou hast now liberty, and needest no mainmission;
> And, if thou aband thee to passions sensual,
> Farewell thy liberty! thou shalt wax thrall.
>
> (p. 48)

The efforts of Sensuality to undermine this hierarchy produce much more lecturing on the same order until he stresses the rôle of free will to bring the controversy to a conclusion:

> This man is put in his own liberty;
> And, certainly, the free choice is his
> Whether he will be governed by thee or by me.
> Let us, therefore, put it to his own jeopardy,
> And therein stand to his arbitrament
> To which of us twain he had liefer assent.
>
> (p. 54)

This early in the struggle, Man chooses Reason to be his chief advisor, of course; and even later, when he is resisting for a moment the full-scale assault of the vices, he shies from their temptations by protesting loyally:

> But I was forbid by Reason
> On mine own fantasy to run,
> Or to take any presumption
> Of mine own wit
>   . . . . . .
> Certain, Nature advised me
> To follow Reason what time that she

> Put me first in authority
> That I stand in now.
>
> (p. 74)

Nevertheless, he chooses his "own fantasy to run" and turns from Reason to an extended life-in-sin. When at last he returns to Reason, he is informed:

> ye must
> Put to your mind and good will
> To be recured of your great excess;
> For, without your help, it cannot be, doubtless!
>
> (p. 121)

Quite central to the basic allegory of this predecessor to *Magnyfycence*, then, are the same psychological commonplaces one finds in Skelton's play.

In *Hyckescorner*, too, the vice who initiates the opposition to the virtues proclaims,

> my name is Frewyll;
> I may chose wheder I do good or yll,
> But, for all that, I wyll do as me lyst.

Such insubordination leads naturally to sin, from which he is rescued only when, at the prompting of the virtues, he turns his wilfulness into its proper channel:

> I wyll not go to the devyll whyle I have my lyberte;
> He shall take the laboure to fet me and he wyl have me!
> For he that wyll go to hell by his wyll voluntary,
> The devyll and the worlewynde go with hym!
> I wyll you never fro thens tydynges brynge;
> Go you before and shewe me the waye,
> And as to folowe you I wyll not saye naye.[12]

---

12. Ll. 159-61, 774-79. *Specimens of the Pre-Shakespearean Drama*, ed. John Matthews Manly (Boston, 1897), I, 391 and 411-12.

But, above all, it is in *Wisdom, Who Is Christ* that psychology is fused with theology to create the central allegory. For, at the very heart of the play, as the title suggests, lies the question posed only subordinately in *Magnyfycence*—what is the proper relationship between reason and will?[13] In true morality fashion, Will's opening soliloquy is self-revelatory:

> Wyll, for dede oft ys take;
>   Therfor þe wyll must weell be dysposyde;
> Than þer begynnyt all grace to wake,
>   Yff with synne yt be not a-nosyde;
>   Therfor þe wyll must be wyll apposyde;
> Or þat yt to þe mevynges yewe consent,
> The lybrary of reson must be wnclosyde
> Ande after hys domys to take entent.

His companions, Mind and Understanding, represent the higher and lower components of the reason whose "domys" should be consulted; but when, in the face of temptation, Will begins to judge the issue by recourse to this reason, Lucifer is quick to reply,

> The wyll of þe soule hath fre dominacion;
> Dyspute not to moche in þis with reson.[14]

Acceptance of this sophistry and the psychological error implied results in the falling away from God by the three "mights," and a return to Christ comes only after the proper relationship has been re-established. Mind's first harken-

---

13. An extensive discussion of these matters may be found in Green, *Medieval Morality*, pp. 48-55. See also, John Joseph Molloy, *A Theological Interpretation of the Moral Play, "Wisdom, Who Is Christ"* (Washington, 1952), pp. 35-47, 65-99, 132-74.
14. Ll. 221-28, 481-82. *The Macro Plays,* ed. Frederick J. Furnivall and Alfred W. Pollard, EETS, ES, XCI (London, 1904), 43 and 51.

ings to Wisdom (who is Christ) are scorned by the lower faculties; only when they follow Mind's inclinations to repent is salvation achieved.

In spite of such analogies from the limited morality survivals, however, Ramsay supposes that "*Magnificence* probably draws its psychology directly from Aristotle, and independently of the earlier plays. . . ."[15] Why it was probably direct borrowing when an entire culture for centuries had exchanged the ideas second and third hand until they had become near-clichés is difficult to follow; but certainly it is true that, whether or not Skelton drew his psychology from the plays, the ideas were not "absolutely novel" ones to them. To view the terms, then, as part of a grand Aristotelian design superimposed upon a morality tradition previously free of it is far to overstate the case.

However, the real strength of Ramsay's interpretation lies not here but in his theory that Measure and Magnyfycence are "distinctively Aristotelian terms." The first of these undoubtedly evokes the Stagirite when one thinks of a "source," though Heiserman shows effectively what common sense would suggest—that the term had long since been generalized beyond any exclusive identity with the *Nicomachean Ethics* (p. 122). I shall delay consideration of the matter until somewhat later in order to confront the main issue—the question of "magnificence" itself.

The *OED* cites two meanings for "magnificence" prevalent during Skelton's age—"sovereign bounty or munificence" and "greatness of name and reputation." Heiserman, citing the occasional usage of the term in earlier drama and

15. P. xxxiv. Earlier, in contradiction, Ramsay had held only that the terms had an Aristotelian origin, "less immediate" (p. xxxii). The lesser claim is by far the more defensible since it is true that the psychology under discussion had been constructed upon Aristotelian foundations (see Anderson, *Elizabethan Psychology*, p. 8).

referring briefly to its widespread use during the era as an epithet denoting glory and greatness,[16] seems to accede to the latter *OED* definition as appropriate to Skelton's intent but to deny the former, thus denying Ramsay's Aristotelian claims, which rest upon an assumption that Skelton intended both meanings and that both come confusedly from the *Ethics*. The denial seems valid, the exact grounds for making it, not so tenable. Both meanings—by all means, the first, with its emphasis upon the handling of wealth by nobility—are present in the play. One need not sacrifice the ironic ambiguity of the king's name to redeem the play from the Aristotelian label so wrenched to fit it; for, as I hope to show, there is another tradition besides the purely Aristotelian one which gives clearer warrant to both meanings without the multiple assumptions of Skelton's confusions which Ramsay is forced to make.

On the one hand, Ramsay must assume that the poet confused Aristotle's "magnificence" with his "liberality":

> Skelton has here adopted the term regularly used to translate the Aristotelian virtue μεγαλοπρέπεια, which is explained in the *Nichomachean Ethics* as signifying suitable expenditure on a large scale (Book IV, Chapters IV.-VI.). In part, however, the conception as it appears in the play answers better to the virtue which Aristotle treats just before magnificence, viz. ἐλευθεριότης, liberality (Chapters I.-III.). The confusion is pardonable, for the two virtues are closely akin, as Aristotle himself declares. Magnificence exceeds liberality in scale; it is the liberality of the great. Doubtless for this reason Skelton selected it as the name of his prince. But Aristotle adds to this distinction that magnificence includes good taste, and accordingly makes it the mean

16. A. R. Heiserman, *Skelton and Satire* (Chicago, [1961]), p. 121. See also p. 86.

between vulgarity on one side and meanness on the other; whereas liberality is a mean between prodigality and illiberality. This element is quite absent from Skelton's conception, which, except for the high rank of its exponent, is exactly the liberality of Aristotle (p. xxxiii).

Such an assumed misreading, though unlikely on the part of a man contemporarily acclaimed for his erudition, is of course possible. But the assumption is unnecessary. Just by reading aright such a work as Thomas Aquinas' *Summa theologica* (and he was contemptuous of those who had not[17]), he would have arrived at the same conclusion. St. Thomas' treatment of the virtues in the *Summa* is not pure Aristotelianism by any means; in fact, it is based fundamentally upon the Ciceronian version of the four cardinal virtues (*prudentia, justitia, fortitudo,* and *temperantia*), to which the ethics of Aristotle and others are subordinately reconciled.[18] It is this ethical tradition of the four virtues that is significant in clarifying Skelton's term. However, to insist that Skelton's Magnyfycence is a "distinctively Thomistic term" would be to make the same error as that implied by claiming it to be a "distinctively Aristotelian" one. The *Summa* is only one of numerous Christian treatises which propagated the doctrine of the cardinal virtues, tried to synthesize it with other systems, and modified and expanded it.[19] Within this influential and well-defined tra-

17. See *A Replycacion Agaynst Certayne Yong Scolers Abiured of Late, &c,* ll. 275-84 (Dyce, *Poetical Works,* I, 217).
18. E. K. Rand, *Cicero in the Courtroom of St. Thomas Aquinas* (Milwaukee, Wis., 1946), pp. 26-32, 103-12.
19. Otto Zöckler, *Die Tugendlehre des Christentums geschichtlich dargestellt in der Entwicklung ihrer Lehrformen, mit besonderer Rücksicht auf deren zahlensymbolische Einkleidung* (Gutersloh, 1904); Catharine Haines, "The Four Greek Virtues from Socrates to Bonaventure," (Master's thesis, Mount Holyoke, 1941); Odon Lottin, "La Théorie des vertus

59

dition—even more narrowly within the concept of Fortitude—most of the characteristics of Skelton's play may be found and the architectonic relationship between its theme and its structure may be understood. For the moment, however, only the definition of Magnyfycence is at issue.

Following Cicero's classification of the four virtues and their subordinates,[20] St. Thomas categorizes magnificence as a part of Fortitude and liberality as a part of Justice. The first difficulty encountered, however, reflects the Aristotelian influence: "Magnificentia enim videtur ad liberalitatem pertinere, quia utraque est circa pecunias" (II-II, Q128).[21] The difficulty is resolved by affirming that magnificence differs only in its addition of a certain greatness (*quandam magnitudem*) to the matter of liberality. Like Skelton, St. Thomas ignores completely the Aristotelian differentia on the basis of vulgarity, the differentia that forces Ramsay to assume Skelton's confusion. Striving always for synthesis, St. Thomas adopts Cicero's definition that "magnificentia est rerum magnarum et excelsarum cum animi ampla quadam et splendida propositione cogitatio atque administratio" (II-II, Q128) but later extends the definition to involve the expenditure of wealth in such a way as to do honor to the whole state (II-II, Q134). The extension reflects the continued Aristotelian pressure upon the Ciceronian definition, which neither contains any such qualification nor

---

cardinales de 1230 à 1250," *Mélanges Mandonnet: Etudies d'histoire littéraire et doctrinale du moyen âge*, II (Paris, 1930) and his *Psychologie et Morale aux XIIe et XIIIe Siècle* (6 vols.; Louvain, 1942-60).

20. *De inventione* ii. 163-64. Skelton, himself, was well acquainted with this second book of Cicero's work, the *locus classicus* of the accepted definitions of the virtues and their parts (including *magnificentia*). See his fourth poem against Garnesche, ll. 8 ff. (Dyce, *Poetical Works*, I, 126). Again in his marginal glosses to *A Replycacion* (*ibid.*, I, 208) he alludes accurately to another portion of the *De inventione*.

21. Throughout, I quote from and cite the *Summa theologica* as edited by the Institute of Mediaeval Studies, 3 vols. (Ottawa, [1941]).

implies any. However, in his more expansive, less codified, discussion of Fortitude in the *De officiis,* Cicero gives clear warrant to the idea by affirming that nothing is more magnificent (*magnificentius*) in the great-souled man "quam pecuniam contemnere, si non habeas, si habeas, ad beneficentiam liberalitatemque conferre."[22]

Like his more renowned scholastic pupil, Albert the Great also associates magnificence with liberality in a way to suggest Skelton's usage. His ethical system, too, is basically ordered upon the Ciceronian plan of the cardinal virtue. Treating Fortitude (with its Ciceronian subordinate, magnificence), he decides that "liberalis est, qui expensam impavidus est. Magnificus autem, qui ad omnem largitionem instupefactibilis."[23] Once again, the distinction is one of degree; magnificence is largess on the grand scale. The differentia as to vulgarity and taste is forgotten as it is in Skelton and St. Thomas. Closer to Skelton's own age and, significantly, within the tradition *de regimine principum* into which *Magnyfycence* might also be included, is Francesco Patrizi's *De regno et regis institvtione,* where, under the cardinal virtue of Fortitude, the author has a chapter on magnificence, in which he says, "Magnificentia locum suum nunc sibi vendical: quae quidem virtus solis Regibus principibus conuenit. Opes enim singulorum vix tanti sunt, vt liberalitatem praestare possint, quae mediocritas quaedam esse debet." Going on to define liberality in the traditional Aristotelian sense, he adds: "Magnificus verò à liberali differt: ille enim circa magna & publica, hic autem circa parua & priuata versatur."[24]

22. i. 20. 68. Citations from the *De officiis* are to the Teubner edition by C. Atzert (Leipzig, 1958).
23. *Ethicorum libros x* iii. 2. 1, in *Opera omnia,* ed. Augustus Borgnet (Paris, 1891), VII, 236a.
24. (Paris, 1578), p. 444^v.

Patrizi's continuation of this tradition is especially revealing in the light of Ramsay's comment that, when in *The Boke Named the Gouernour* Sir Thomas Elyot "gives the distinction between liberality and magnificence, he fails just as Skelton does to make magnificence include good taste" (p. lxxvii). The assumption of Elyot's "failure," like that of Skelton's "confusion," is not at all necessary if one keeps in mind that Elyot's work is largely ordered upon the plan of the four virtues, and that he follows Cicero and even Patrizi himself as well as Aristotle.[25] Out of this kind of mélange no less than out of the more disciplined scholastic efforts at synthesis, the concept of magnificence as liberality on a more exalted level repeatedly occurs, with the doctrine of the cardinal virtues always a basic factor.

If this tradition offers a more probable explanation of Skelton's use of magnificence as meaning princely liberality than does an hypothesis that he misread Aristotle, there still remains an assumption that the poet was further confused. For Ramsay adds:

> When . . . Magnificence is used for nobility or greatness in general, we apparently have another confusion, this

---

25. The question as to the amount and kind of reliance Elyot placed upon his various sources (especially Patrizi) is a matter of some disagreement; however, for the purposes of the present discussion the exact nature of the indebtednesses is not a significant one since the matter of individual influence is not as relevant as is that of the continuity of a tradition. The shifting of scholarly opinion on the matter of Elyot's sources can be followed in H. H. Croft's edition of *The Boke Named the Gouernour* (2 vols.; London, 1883); Josef Schlotter, "Thomas Elyots 'Governour' in seinem Verhältnis zu Francesco Patrizi" (Ph.D. dissertation, Freiburg, 1938); Leslie Clare Warren, *Humanistic Doctrines of the Prince from Petrarch to Sir Thomas Elyot: A Study of the Principal Analogues and Sources of "The Boke Named the Governour"* (Chicago, 1939), and "Patrizi's *De Regno et Regis Institutione* and the Plan of Elyot's *The Boke Named the Governour*," *JEGP*, XLIX (1950), 67-77; Stanford E. Lehmberg, *Sir Thomas Elyot, Tudor Humanist* (Austin, Texas, 1960), pp. 72-94.

time with the Aristotelian μεγαλοψυχία, magnanimity (Chapters VII.-IX.), which, as Aristotle says, shows the possession of such greatness as belongs to every virtue. This is due, however, less to the mistake of the poet than to the change of the language, which had long before (see *N.E.D.* 3) generalized the word. But the double usage of the word by Skelton is interesting in view of the unquestionable mistake made later by Spenser in his introductory letter to the *Faërie Queene,* when he says: "In the person of Arthur, I sette forth magnificence in particular, which virtue for that (according to Aristotle and the rest) it is the perfection of all the rest, and containeth in it them all" (see Jusserand, "Spenser's Twelve Private Morall Vertues," *Mod. Phil.* III. 373-384). Spenser in all probability owes the name Colin Clout to Skelton's satire by that title; and it is not impossible that he was misled by the ambiguous usage of Skelton's morality (p. xxxiii).

The incidental postulation that Spenser may have inadvertently followed Skelton's error in making his own "unquestionable mistake" in the letter to the *Faerie Queene* provides a convenient entry to the whole problem. For it indicates once again to what extent modern scholarship has advanced since the writing of this interpretation. The article by Jusserand was merely the first of a series of studies which, if they left inconclusive the original question of explaining Spenser's designation of "twelve," served to call attention to the fact that Aristotle's views, as known to the sixteenth century, had often been greatly modified by the incrustations of innumerable medieval commentators and by the mergings with other systems of ethics.[26] By far the

26. J. J. Jusserand, "Spenser's 'Twelve Private Morall Vertues as Aristotle Hath Devised,'" *MP*, III (1906), 373-83; William Fenn De Moss, "Spenser's Twelve Moral Virtues 'According to Aristotle,'" *MP*, XVI (1918),

most prominent of these systems that stand between pure Aristotelianism and the ethical patterns of the *Faerie Queene* has been shown by these studies to be that of the four cardinal virtues. Indeed, Jusserand's major thesis was that Spenser's plan reflects, not pure Aristotelianism, but a vital tradition deriving twelve virtues from the four cardinal ones. This Christian-Stoic system, if not the precise treatise advanced by Jusserand, has increasingly been shown by scholars to account for many of the non-Aristotelian concepts found in the epic.[27]

One recent study in particular bears directly upon the question at issue in that it demonstrates Spenser's magnificence to be not an "unquestionable mistake" for magnanimity but a reflection of Thomas Aquinas' partial fusion of the two terms in the *Summa theologica*.[28] Thus, Spenser need neither have misread Aristotle nor have been "misled by the ambiguous usage of Skelton's morality." Indeed, if this explanation is valid, there is no unintended ambiguity in Skelton's usage either. To demonstrate its validity I

23-38, 245-70 [also published as *The Influence of Aristotle's "Politics" and "Ethics" on Spenser* (Chicago, [1920])]; H. S. V. Jones, "The Faerie Queene and the Mediaeval Aristotelian Tradition," *JEGP*, XXV (1926), 283-98, and "Magnanimity in Spenser's Legend of Holiness," *SP*, XXIX (1932), 200-6; Viola Blackburn Hulbert, "Spenser's Twelve Moral Virtues 'According to Aristotle and the Rest,'" *University of Chicago Abstracts of Theses, Humanistic Series*, V (1926), 479-85; Josephine Waters Bennett, *The Evolution of the Faerie Queene* (Chicago, [1942]), pp. 216-30. Selected portions of many of these studies can be found in *The Works of Edmund Spenser: A Variorum Edition*, ed. Edwin Greenlaw et al., I (Baltimore, 1932), 314-62.

27. In addition to both articles by Jones and Mrs. Bennett's chapter cited in the note above, see especially Viola Blackburn Hulbert's "A Possible Christian Source for Spenser's Temperance," *SP*, XXVIII (1931), 184-210, which shows that the cardinal virtue of Temperance provides a far better gloss to Book II than does Aristotle's virtue, long assumed to be the ethical model misconstrued by Spenser.

28. Michael F. Moloney, "St. Thomas and Spenser's Virtue of Magnificence," *JEGP*, LII (1953), 58-62.

shall examine the pertinent section of the *Summa*, paralleling to some extent the article just cited.

The first thing to be noticed is that the context out of which St. Thomas' discussion arises is the same referred to earlier in resolving the magnificence-liberality complex—that is, his treatment of Fortitude, the cardinal virtue, basically Ciceronian but modified by Aristotelianism. In defining the virtue he subdivides Cicero's four component parts (confidence, magnificence, patience, and perseverance) into two categories, the aggressive and the enduring. For the first category, he designates confidence and magnificence, as companion and complementary virtues, and immediately substitutes for the former " 'magnanimitas' . . . quae videtur idem esse fiduciae."[29] This substitution he thereafter makes a permanent one, beginning his next question, for instance, "Deinde considerandum est de singulis fortitudinis partibus, ita tamen quod sub quatuor principalibus quas Tullius ponit, alias comprehendamus; nisi quod magnanimitatem, de qua

29. II-II, Q128. St. Thomas' substitution is seen to be not purely arbitrary when viewed in the fuller perspective of his efforts to synthesize the various lists of subordinate parts to the virtue to which his age was the puzzled heir. Confronted not only by Cicero's list of four (*fiducia, magnificentia, patientia, perseverantia*) but by Macrobius' seven (*magnanimitas, fiducia, securitas, magnificentia, constantia, tolerantia, firmitas*) as well as by another list of seven by Andronicus of Rhodes, he insists that Cicero's is most basic and reconciles the other two lists to it, virtue by virtue. In the process of the synthesis, he observes that Macrobius adds three extra subvirtues, "Quorum duo, scilicet magnanimitas et securitas, a Tullio sub fiducia comprehenduntur; sed Macrobius magis per specialia distinguit. Nam fiducia importat spem hominis ad magna. Spes autem cuiuslibet rei praesupponit appetitum in magna protensum per desiderium, quod pertinet ad magnanimitatem; dictum est enim supra quod spes praesupponit amorem et desiderium rei speratae. Vel potest melius dici quod fiducia pertinet ad spei certitudinem; magnanimitas autem ad magnitudinem rei speratae." On the basis of this analysis, he makes the substitution noted, thus opening the way for consideration of Aristotelian magnanimity in the context of the cardinal virtues, which are not Aristotelian at all.

etiam Aristoteles tractat, loco fiduciae ponemus" (II-II, Q129). As in the case of the magnificence-liberality relationship, the basically Ciceronian version of the cardinal virtue is modified by the *Nicomachean Ethics* to produce an affinity of terms like that Ramsay is forced to consider to be the result of Skelton's confusion. Whether the matter be one of confusion, distortion, or extremely subtle refinement, the credit or blame probably lies, not with Skelton, but with an ethical synthesizer like St. Thomas, whose basic referent is the system of the four cardinal virtues.

The affinity established between magnificence and magnanimity within the *Summa theologica* goes even further than that just noted. Developing a distinction that glorious deeds are conceived by magnanimity and executed by magnificence, St. Thomas practically makes the two interchangeable by giving each something of the power of the other:

> Dicendum quod ad magnanimitatem pertinent non solum tendere in magnum, sed etiam "in omnibus virtutibus magnum operari", vel faciendo vel qualitercumque, agendo, ut dicitur in IV *Eth.* . . . .
> . . . .
> Ad magnificentiam vero pertinent non solum facere magnum secundum quod facere proprie sumitur, sed etiam ad magnum faciendum tendere animo; unde Tullius dicit . . . , quod "magnificentia est rerum magnarum et excelsarum, cum animi quadam ampla et splendida propositione, cogitatio atque administratio"; ut cogitatio referatur ad interiorem intentionem, administratio autem ad exteriorem executionem. Unde oportet quod sicut magnanimitas intendit aliquod magnum in omni materia, ita et magnificentia in aliquo opere factibili (II-II, Q134, a2).

The fact that each term is so carefully related to the etymology of the other (*magnanimitas* to *magnum facere*, and *magnificentia* to *magnus animus*) suggests how deliberate was the effort to consider them synonymous.

The tradition of the four cardinal virtues, impinged upon here by Thomas' new Aristotelianism, offers then a much more likely source for Skelton's (and Spenser's) use of magnificence in the sense of magnanimity than does the *Nicomachean Ethics*, even misread. When, further, it is recalled that this resolution comes from the identical chapters of the same work where can be found an alternative to the other supposed confusion (between liberality and magnificence), one must reject the old theory as far too tenuous.

However, lest it appear that "distinctively Thomistic terms" are merely being substituted for Aristotelian ones, it should be observed again that the *Summa,* while one of the fullest, is only one of many works on the cardinal virtues which indicate a fusion of these terms. For example, Guilielmus Peraldus cites and defines Cicero's magnificence as a part of Fortitude and follows it with the terse observation: "Nec loquitur de magnanimitate: immo sub magnificentia comprehendit eam."[30] It really makes little difference whether, as seems the case, Thomas of Sutton (*ca.* 1300) is reflecting the Aquinian view in referring to the "propinquitatem habendi istas uirtutes (magnificentie et magnanimitatis)"[31] and Vincent of Beauvais, the Peraldian one by alluding to "magnificentia siue magnanimitas."[32] Far more relevant to our purposes is the evidence provided by such allusions that the interrelationship of the two terms within the context of the cardinal virtues had come to be viewed as a truth requiring only passing affirmation.

30. *Summa de virtutibus et vitiis* (Basle, 1497), I. iii. 4. 10.
31. As quoted by Lottin, *Psychologie et Morale*, III, 250.
32. *Speculum doctrinale* ([Strassburg, *ca.* 1470]), V. lxxii.

The affinity thus established by scholasticism permeated *belles lettres* as well. Gower, admired and emulated by Skelton, reflects the tradition when, in discussing magnanimity as one of the daughters of Fortitude, he says:

> Iceste file ad sa compaigne,
> Q'en tous les oeveres l'acompaine,
> Magnificence est appellée,
> Tant sont ce deux de vertu plaine,
> N'est riens q'encontre lour remaine
> Que par labour n'est conquestée:
> Car n'est vertu d'ascun degré
> Dont ceste Magnanimité
> Commencer n'ose l'overaigne;
> Et qant la chose est commencée,
> Ja n'ert si forte honnesteté
> Qe l'autre a son droit fin ne maine.[33]

Or to enter the dramatist's own age, one might cite Alexander Barclay's synonymous uses of the terms in his translation of and expansion upon the *De quatuor virtutibus* of Dominicus Mancinus.[34] Later in the century, Lodowick Bryskett struggles to keep feet in both Ciceronian and Aristotelian camps and, like Thomas Aquinas, says first that "Vnto liberality is ioyned magnificence" and almost immediately says also that "Arme in arme with Magnificence goeth Magnanimity."[35] On the other hand, Pierre de la Primaudaye, in *The French Academie,* is more Peraldian

33. *Mirour de l'Omme,* ll. 14245-56, in *The Complete Works of John Gower,* ed. G. C. Macaulay (Oxford, 1899), I, 165.
34. *Here begynnyth a treatyse intitulyd the myrrour of good maners conteynynge the .iiii. vertues callyd cardynall compyled in latyn by Domynike Mancyn* ([London, *ca.* 1517]), [Dvi]^v-Eiii^v.
35. *A Discovrse of Civill Life: Containing the Ethike part of Morall Philosophie. Fit for the instructing of a Gentleman in the course of a vertuous life* (London, 1606), p. 223.

in identifying "Magnanimitie . . . as that which vndoubtedly is comprehended vnder the first part of *Fortitude,* which *Cicero* calleth Magnificence."[36]

Whether in the Aquinian or the Peraldian stream, whether receiving scholarly or popular expression, whether explicit or implied, the tradition finds unity in wedding magnificence to magnanimity as Ramsay finds Skelton to do in his morality. Both the assumed confusions on the dramatist's part, then, are resolved instead into an accurate reliance upon an extremely vital tradition, that of the cardinal virtue, Fortitude, within whose context the term, magnificence, developed a flexible association with both liberality and magnanimity like that apparent also in Skelton's usage.

Indeed, this flexibility occasionally went even farther. La Primaudaye, for instance, identifying magnanimity with magnificence, as noted above, then makes the former synonymous with Fortitude itself (pp. 328, 349, 389, etc.). Similarly, in translating Mancinus, Barclay smoothly interchanges all three terms (Bi^r and Diii^v-[Eiv]^r). Giraldus Cambrensis had been more direct, beginning his chapter "De principis magnificentia" by referring to "Magnificentia vero, quae et fortitudo dicitur," [37] just as Gerard Legh was to begin his analysis by affirming that "Fortitude is magnificence."[38] In fact, this is the tradition followed by Skelton's model poet, John Lydgate, who speaks of "Fortitudo, / Whame philosophres by þeyre sentence/ Ar wonte to cleepe Magnyfysence."[39]

The significance of this ultimate identity of magnificence with the cardinal virtue itself lies in the fact that this more

36. Trans. T. B[owes] (London, 1586), p. 289.
37. *Opera, Vol. VIII: De principis instructione liber,* ed. George F. Warner ("Roll Series," 2d set, XXI [London, 1891]), p. 30.
38. *The Accedens of Armory* (London, 1568), [A6]^v.
39. Henry Noble MacCracken, ed., *The Minor Poems of John Lydgate, Part II: Secular Poems,* EETS, OS, CXCII (London, 1934), 688.

inclusive virtue (seen in the present chapter to resolve the problems posed by Skelton's central allegorical term) was defined before, during, and after Skelton's day in a manner that closely accords with the full dramatic action of the play. A comparative study of this definition and the play's structure in the following chapter will carry us a long way toward redeeming the morality from the rather truncated view forced upon it as much by the Aristotelian interpretation of its theme as by the Wolseyan satire the theme was alleged to have served.

4 · Fortitude and the Two-Part Morality Structure

Up to Skelton's day, the English morality play had evolved conservatively into a very limited variety of structural patterns, the most popular of which was the "conflict" design suitable for dramatizing the struggle of good and evil forces for the soul of man. Basic to this species, and seldom modified, was the pattern that dictated two struggles, in the first of which the hitherto innocent representative of mankind is entrapped into sin and in the second of which, after an interlude of dissolute living, he is rescued from his career of vice and set upon the path of regeneration. *Wisdom, Who Is Christ* and *Mankynde,* as well as the morality portion of *Mary Magdalen,* all follow this sequence. *Hyckescorner* differs only in that, since there is no human figure to be won or lost, there is no life-in-sin interlude between conflicts, only a lament by a virtue defeated in the first encounter. *Nature* and *The Nature of the Four Elements* follow the conventional pattern and then repeat the sequence a second time. *The Castle of Perseverance* develops along the same lines, but in the second sequence the final conflict is replaced by the motif of the four daughters of God, debating over the soul of Humanus Genus, who has died in sin. Finally, only the author's dramatic implication of original sin prevents *Mundus et infans* from following the basic design, and even so its departure from the norm is minimal. With humanity entrapped by sin at the outset, an initial conversion is needed; thereafter the structure is conventional—a temptation into sin and, after an interlude, a redemption from sin.

This structural legacy Skelton inherited and perpetuated almost unchanged in his own morality, whose conventional two struggles embody the successive and alternate temptations—first in prosperity, then in adversity—which Magnyfycence undergoes as do so many of his predecessors. However, the question of the play's artistic integrity rests upon whether the dramatist, in using the form in its full scope, did so to embody a pattern of ideas that could be dramatically served by the dual-conflict motif his Tudor audience had probably come unconsciously to expect in a morality play, or whether his fidelity to the form leads him into slavish imitation of its latter stages even though the theme he develops has been accomplished in terms of the first conflict alone. If it is the latter, the architectonic failure is a serious one. Even the authors of *The Castle of Perseverance* and of *Mundus et infans* are not so tyrannized by the conventional structure as to follow it by rote to the jeopardy of their theological purposes; each adapts form to content. The Aristotelian theme claimed for *Magnyfycence,* however, leads to just such an assumption that Skelton blindly wrote out the last seven hundred lines of his play, including an entirely irrelevant second conflict, in slavish obedience to a morality structure that no longer suited his thematic purposes. On the other hand, theme and structure remain congruent throughout when one understands the ethics of the play to derive from the same cardinal virtue of Fortitude, sometimes called Magnificence or Magnanimity, already shown to suggest usages of the term "magnificence" analogous to Skelton's.

In interpreting the play as dramatizing a theme of Aristotelian magnificence or liberality, not only must we assume Skelton's misreading of his source and his artistic unconcern for the architectonics of his play but we must recognize as well that he would be drawing upon only half of the doctrine from the *Nicomachean Ethics*. For there Aristotle holds liberality to be a virtuous mean between two extremes, avarice as well as prodigality. But in Skelton's play avarice plays no significant part at all. Prodigal conduct is, to be sure, an important factor in the opening struggle; but the second conflict deals not with avarice, as one might expect if the play were basically Aristotelian, but with despair and suicide in adversity, about which Aristotle says nothing. Mentioned in passing only once in the entire play (ll. 2488-89), avarice as the defect of liberality plays no part at all in the dramatic action.

While an Aristotelian reading of *Magnyfycence* must lead to a conclusion that the play is at best an imbalanced, only partial dramatization of a misunderstood dogma, the tradition of the cardinal virtues had come by Skelton's day to offer the identical pattern of ideas—resistance to the temptations of adversity as well as of prosperity—which Skelton's morality allegorizes in terms of the conventional dual-conflict motif of its genre. Practically from the beginning, in the germinal works of both Cicero and Macrobius, there began to emerge in discussions of the four virtues a concept that by Fortitude one resisted the temptations posed by these alternately extreme conditions of life. Cicero, for instance, admonishes at one point in the *De officiis:* "Etiam in rebus prosperis et ad voluntatem nostram fluentibus superbiam magnopere, fastidium arrogantiamque fugiamus. Nam ut

73

adversas res, sic secundas immoderate ferre levitatis est praeclaraque est aequabilitas in omni vita" (i. 26. 90). To this it might be well to relate the passage previously observed from Cicero's discussion of magnificence in Fortitude (see above, p. 61). When he says that "nihil ... magnificentius ... quam pecuniam contemnere, si non habeas, si habeas, ad beneficentiam liberalitatemque conferre," he does so with an understanding that Fortitude strengthens one against both prosperity and adversity. For he has just observed, "Nam et ea, quae eximia plerisque et praeclara videntur, parva ducere eaque ratione stabili firmaque contemnere fortis animi magnique ducendum est, et ea, quae videntur acerba, quae multa et varia in hominum vita fortunaque versantur, ita ferre, ut nihil a statu naturae discedas, nihil a dignitate sapientis, robusti animi est magnaeque constantiae. Non est autem consentaneum, qui metu non frangatur, eum frangi cupiditate, nec qui invictum se a labore praestiterit, vinci a voluptate" (i. 20. 67-68). As in Skelton's play, liberality is a virtue appropriate to prosperity but is only part of the attribute of one whose fuller purpose is to achieve *aequabilitatem in omni vita*.

While the intermittent influence of the *De officiis* throughout the early centuries of the middle ages[1] served to propagate this concept to some extent as Cicero expressed

1. N. E. Nelson, "Cicero's *De Officiis* in Christian Thought: 300-1300," *Essays and Studies in English and Comparative Literature* ("University of Michigan Publications, Language and Literature," X [Ann Arbor, 1933]), 59-160; Hans Baron, "Cicero and the Roman Civic Spirit in the Middle Ages and Early Renaissance," *Bulletin of the John Rylands Library*, XXII (1938), 72-97; Ralph Graham Palmer, *Seneca's "De Remediis Fortvitorvm" and the Elizabethans* . . . (Chicago, 1953), pp. 7-18. For a depreciation of Cicero's direct influence during the middle ages, see Ernst Robert Curtius, *European Literature and the Latin Middle Ages*, trans. Willard R. Trask ("Bollingen Series," XXXVI [New York, 1953]), p. 523, where he cites Schanz-Hosius, *Römische Literaturgeschichte*, I⁴ (1927), 546.

it, it received probably its greatest impetus, and some disproportionate emphasis, from its absorption into the emerging Christian ethics. For St. Ambrose, in patterning his *De officiis ministrorum* on its Ciceronian namesake, gave the idea even more prominence than had his model. At one point, he declares, "Et re vera jure ea fortitudo vocatur, quando unusquisque . . . nullis illecebris emollitur atque inflectitur, non adversis perturbatur, non extollitur secundis."[2] The next chapter, entitled "Servandam ut in prosperis, ita et in adversis mentis, aequalitatem," begins a further development of the interpretation by observing, "Ea est etiam quae dicitur vacuitas animi ab angoribus; ut neque in doloribus molliores simus, neque in prosperis elatiores" (i. 37. 185). He even comes back to it again by starting a later chapter, "Verum quia fortitudo non solum secundis rebus, sed etiam adversis probatur" (i. 41. 199).

This emphasis by Ambrose upon an idea that Cicero had initiated but not so stressed gained for the concept a much more central position in subsequent discussions of the virtue. Isidore of Seville, for example, seems to have the wording of Ambrose in mind when he affirms that "Fortitudo . . . nullis emollitur illecebris, adversis non frangitur, non elevatur secundis."[3] Thus given repeated sanction in those

2. I. 36. 180. Citations from the *De officiis ministrorum* in my text are to *PL*, XVI; the work has been translated by Rev. H. De Romestin, *Some of the Principal Works of St. Ambrose*, in *A Select Library of Nicene and Post-Nicene Fathers of the Christian Church*, 2nd Ser., ed. Philip Schaff and Henry Wace, X (New York, 1896), 1-89.

3. *Differentiarum, sive De propietate sermonum*, ii. 39. 157 (*PL*, LXXXIII, 95). See, also, Simon of Tournai, who specifically cites the *De officiis* before saying "non frangatur aduersis uel extollatur prosperis, quod exigit fortitudo. Siue enim frangatur aduersis siue non, siue extollatur prosperis siue non, si tamen mens bona constitutione habilis est ut, si emergat aduersistas uel prosperitas, nec frangatur aduersis nec extollatur prosperis, dicitur habitu habere fortitudinem" as cited in Odon Lottin, *Psychologie et Morale aux XII*[e] *et XIII*[e] *Siècle* (6 vols.; Louvain, 1942-60), III, 107, 108.

works of the church fathers destined to influence the emerging Christian ethics of medieval Europe, the concept continued to flourish apart. When the direct influence of the *De officiis* re-established itself through the *Moralium dogma philosophorum* and those treatises that borrowed from it, it is not surprising that Fortitude was by then often defined in terms reminiscent of the selected and emphasized passages from Cicero. Peraldus, who speaks (as noticed earlier) of "Magnanimitas que et fortitudo dicitur," follows this passage with one that defines the virtue by referring to Cicero's "Non est autem consentanteum, qui metu non frangatur, eum frangi cupiditate nec."[4] Even more directly, Vincent of Beauvais develops his major chapter on Fortitude by means of the definition that "Fortitudo est virtus que nec adversitatis incursu frangitur: nec blandimento prosperitatis eleuatur."[5]

By this point, the Ciceronian strand has become too entangled with the Macrobian, the Senecan, and others to allow or even necessitate tracing its separate course. What can be suggested is the extent to which Cicero's text had come to be read, by Skelton's day, as epitomizing the prosperity-adversity dualism to which medievalism had so often reduced it. For in the first English translation of the *De officiis* in 1534, Robert Whittinton introduces at the proper point a marginal gloss that succinctly defines Fortitude as that virtue which gives man "contempt bothe of prosperyte and

4. *Summa de virtutibus et vitiis* (Basle, 1497), I. iii. 4. 9.
5. *Speculum doctrinale* ([Strassburg, 1470]), V. lxxi. See also Brunetto Latini, *Li Livres dou Tresor*, ed. Francis J. Carmody ("University of California Publications in Modern Philology," XXII [Berkeley, 1948]), 269, where one of the sub-virtues of Fortitude is said "a retenir fermeté en l'une fortune et en l'autre, si ke l'om se s'eshauce trop par prosperité, et ne soit trop troublés en adversité, mais tiegne le mi" (II. lxxxviii).
6. *The thre bookes of Tullyes offyces, bothe in latyne tonge & in englysshe, lately translated by Roberte Whytinton poete laureate* (London, 1534), sig. D6r.

aduersyte."⁶ That Whittinton was Skelton's friend, eulogist, fellow laureate, and Trojan ally in the grammarians' war⁷ suggests to some extent at least how close the dramatist was to this traditional reading of Cicero. Far more suggestive even is the fact that the surviving copy of the *De officiis* and commentary that Henry VIII studied as a prince allegedly under the tutelage of Skelton himself has marked for special emphasis the passage cited earlier in which Cicero says, "Nam ut adversas res, sic secundas immoderate ferre levitatis est praeclaraque est aequabilitas in omni vita."⁸

However, as provocative as such things are, it is well to recall that this pattern of ideas was not restricted to the Ciceronian source alone but was part of the larger ethical heritage of the four cardinal virtues as they descended to medieval Europe from other sources as well. Macrobius, no less than Cicero, gave rise to the concept; in fact, it occupies a more central place and receives more explicit formulation in his treatment of Fortitude than it does in Cicero's. Skelton, who alludes knowingly to "Macrobius that did trete / Of Scipions dreme what was the treu probate," would have read there too that Fortitude requires rulers of commonwealths "tolare fortiter uel aduersa uel

7. William Nelson, *John Skelton, Laureate* (New York, 1939), pp. 148-57; and Ian A. Gordon, *John Skelton, Poet Laureate* (Melbourne, 1943), pp. 34-36.
8. *Commentum familiare in Ciceronis officia, cum Petri Marsi exactissima explanatione* . . . ([Lyon], 1502), fol. LXVIIIʳ. The copy of the text in question is one marked on the first page "Thys Boke is Myne Prynce Henry" and now in the Folger Shakespeare Library. See the "Report from the Folger Library," X:1 (April 22, 1961), 8. It should be noted that Skelton's tutoring of Henry beyond 1502 (the date of publication of the volume in question) is not a matter of unanimous agreement. Nelson presents a circumstantial case that Skelton did not remain tutor long after the death of Prince Arthur in 1502 (*Skelton*, pp. 74-75); however, more recently Peter Green has found the evidence inconclusive, in his pamphlet *John Skelton* (London, 1960), p. 17.

prospera."⁹ Even if he had not actually read the commentary on the *Somnium,* he could hardly have avoided the Macrobian influence; for the eighth chapter of the commentary (in which the cardinal virtue system is expounded) was one of the most influential of all the chapters upon Christian culture. It became a *locus classicus* for the definitions of the virtues, to be drawn upon by such writers as St. Bonaventure, Vincent of Beauvais, Albert the Great, St. Thomas Aquinas, and others.[10]

A derivative compiler like Peraldus would record Macrobius' very words upon prosperity and adversity at one point (I. iii. 4. 2) and cite Cicero's at another (I. iii. 4. 9). Merging in such synthetic works, the two parallel traditions lay ready at hand to influence and become a part of that flood of religious instruction manuals that originated from Archbishop Peckham's Lambeth Canons (1281) and derived their ethical patterns from Peraldus' *Summa.*[11] As a consequence, in a representative work such as *The Lay Folks' Catechism* (1357) appears the definition, "Fortitudo constat

9. *Commentarius in somnium Scipionis,* i. 8. 7. Citations from Macrobius in my text are to the edition of his works by Franz E. Eyssenhardt (2nd ed.; Leipzig, 1893). The *Somnium* has been translated by William H. Stahl, *Commentary on the Dream of Scipio* ("Records of Civilization, Sources and Studies," XLVIII [New York, 1952]). Skelton's eulogy of Macrobius is from the *Garlande of Laurell,* ll. 367-68 (*The Poetical Works of John Skelton,* ed. Rev. Alexander Dyce [2 vols.; London, 1843], I, 376).

10. Philip M. Schedler, *Die Philosophie des Macrobius und ihr Einfluss auf die Wissenschaft des christlichen Mittelalters,* in *Beiträge zur Geschichte der Philosophie des Mittelalters,* XIII :1 (Münster, 1916), pp. 140-57.

11. For a study of the whole phenomenon of the Canons, the instructional manuals, and the relationship of Peraldus to them, see H. G. Pfander, "Some Medieval Manuals of Religious Instruction in England and Observations on Chaucer's Parson's Tale," *JEGP,* XXXV (1936), 243-58; and Gerald Robert Owst, *Preaching in Medieval England: An Introduction to Sermon Manuscripts of the Period, c. 1350-1450* (Cambridge, England, 1926), pp. 279-92.

in prosperis et adversis aquanimiter tolerandis," which is expanded in the authorized metrical translation so that the virtue is said to enable one,

Euenly to sofir the wele and the wa,
Welthe or wandreth, whethir so betides,
And that our hert be noght to hegh for no welefare,
Ne ouer mikel undir for nane yvel fare.[12]

The Macrobian stream, then, was as rich and as influential as the Ciceronian and by this time inseparable from it. Alongside them both during the earlier middle ages had flowed such tributaries as Cassiodorus ("Contra adversa vel prospera remedialis opponitur fortitudo"[13]), Gregory the Great ("fortitudo est . . . prosperitatis blandimenta contemnere, adversitatis metum in corde superare"[14]), and Hrabanus Maurus ("per fortitudinem vero omne quod [rex] provide perspexerit, sive adversa sive prospera"[15]). Their unanimity testifies to an extremely vital ethical tradition; and the confluence of all the branches into the scholastic synthesis, as well as the later humanistic return to the basic resources of antiquity, led to even more expansive discussions of the concept in the years nearer to Skelton's own.

However, before noticing such developments and com-

12. John de Thoresby, *The Lay Folks' Catechism*, ed. T. F. Simmons and H. E. Nolloth, EETS, OS, CXVIII (London, 1901), 84 and 86. The exceedingly popular, corrupted version known as *Don Jon Gaytryge's Sermon* has been edited by G. G. Perry, *Religious Pieces in Prose and Verse*, EETS, OS, XXVI (2nd ed.; London, 1914), p. 11. Similarly, Dan Michel's *Ayenbite of Inwyt*, ed. Richard Morris, EETS, OS, XXIII (London, 1866), instructs that the man who has Fortitude, "Aduerseté and prosperité he berþ and þoleþ wyþ-oute wepinge. ne ariʒthalf ne alefthalf" (p. 125).

13. *De anima*, v (*PL*, LXX, 1290).

14. *Moralium libri*, ii. 7. 21 (*PL*, LXXV, 778).

15. *De anima* (*PL*, CX, 1118). See also, H. O. Taylor, *The Mediaeval Mind* (4th ed.; London, 1938), I, 297-98; as well as Alanus de Insulis, *Summa de arte praedicatoria*, xxiv (*PL*, CCX, 159-60).

paring them to the basic allegorical pattern that gives form to *Magnyfycence,* I would call attention, in passing, to a variant of the tradition. This alternate interpretation seems to have arisen from a passage in the influential eleventh-century *De spiritu et animi* (wrongly attributed to Augustine), which reads: "Habet [anima] virtutes, quibus instruitur et armatur contra vitia: . . . temperantiam habet contra prospera; fortitudinem contra adversa" (*PL,* XL, 794). This alignment, involving two of the cardinal virtues instead of Fortitude alone, was subscribed to by Chancellor Philippe, Alexander of Hales, Jean de la Rochelle, and others[16] and found its way into popular literature through the manuals of religious instruction. For example, among the manuals deriving from Archbishop Peckham's edict, there were those like the *Speculum ecclesiae,* which reflected this variant of the tradition just as *The Lay Folks' Catechism* embodied the one relating Fortitude alone to the temptations of prosperity and adversity. Manuals such as the former taught the devout that "there be .ii. thynges that letteth a man to do good and to leue the yll, that is to wyte, the prosperyte of this worlde that deceueth hym by flatery, pleasures, & fals swetenesse, & the aduersyte of the same that may oppresse by the sorrowfull & sore sharpnesse & paynes. Therfore agaynst prosperyte ye must haue measure and dyscrecyon that ye be not to moche elate & proude of it, & this vertue is called temperaunce. And agaynst aduersyteye ye must haue audacyte, or boldenesse that ye be not ouercome and cast out [and that is called fortitude]."[17]

16. Lottin, *Psychologie et Morale,* III, 159-71 *passim.*
17. I quote from *The Myrrour of the Chyrche,* trans. Robert Copland (London, 1527), Cii^r, because, as first edited in 1521, it represents a version most nearly approximating the time of *Magnyfycence.* There are various modern editions of the many versions (in prose and meter and

Except for its extension to involve two instead of a single cardinal virtue, the principle is the same as that founded more classically upon Cicero and Macrobius. The two versions easily co-existed, any distinction between them being so blurred or disregarded that both sometimes appear in the same work.[18] Between the two, every major discussion of the four virtues down to Skelton's day, with the single important exception of Martin of Braga's *Formula vitae honestae* (*ca.* 570), afforded a reader some acquaintance with an ethical dogma that a man should resist the extreme temptations of prosperity and adversity, which alternately are the very temptations faced by Skelton's play-king. As apparent from the excerpts cited from the manuals of instructions of the late middle ages, these discussions tended to become somewhat more discursive after the scholastic period of synthesis, the terse pronouncements of church fathers and medieval clerics being embroidered and developed with specific details as to the nature of the temptations and modes of conduct. The treachery of flattery and of pleasures, the lure of wealth, and especially the inclination of the heart to be "to hegh," to be "to moche elate & proud" in times of prosperity were specifically suggested as was the inclination of a man to be "ouer mikel undir," to be unduely oppressed by "the sorrowfull & sore sharpnesse & paynes" of adversity. As in *Magnyfycence,* what was needed to resist these temptations was "measure and

under various titles) of Edmund Rich's original *Speculum ecclesiae.* See *Yorkshire Writers: Richard Rolle of Hampole, an English Father of the Church and His Followers,* ed. Carl Horstmann (London, 1895), I, 228-49; Perry, ed., *Religious Pieces in Prose and Verse,* pp. 29-30; *The Minor Poems of the Vernon MS, Part I,* ed. Carl Horstmann, EETS, OS, XCVIII (London, 1892), pp. 248 and 281.

The final bracketed clause in the passage I cite is added marginally in a later hand, but it does correspond to such concluding and balancing phrasings in other versions of the *Speculum.*

18. As, for example, in Peraldus, I. iii. 4. 2 and I. iii. 4. 4.

dyscrecyon," the capacity "euenly to sofir" either condition of life.

Nor were such discussions confined solely, or even primarily, to religious channels (where, as a priest proud of his theological readings, Skelton would repeatedly have found them); they appeared as well in the very "royal handbooks" Ramsay cites as containing analogues to the dramatist's treatment of liberality and prodigality. For instance, the passages paralleled from Hoccleve's *Regement of Prynces* (pp. lxxiii-lxxv), while undeniably akin to Skelton's dramatization of prodigality and its consequences, are actually taken from a larger context, which must be understood before this subordinate part of it can be accurately appreciated. The doctrinal heart of the *Regement,* exclusive of its medieval introductory vision of the beggar and his advice to the poet, is structured about four major "chapters" on each of the cardinal virtues, to which are subordinated various sections treating ideas conventionally associated with the respective virtues.[19] One such major "chapter," entitled "De Regis Magnanimitate" (l. 3900, p. 141), is followed by three sub-divisions, one of which ("De Virtute Largitatis, & Vicio Prodigalitatis" [l. 4124, p. 149]), contains the parallels noted by Ramsay. The fundamental chapter on Magnanimity or Fortitude opens with a familiar definition of the virtue:

19. Lester K. Born, in the introduction to his translation of Erasmus, *The Education of a Christian Prince* (New York, 1936), p. 122, cites Hoccleve's lines, "Prudence, attemperancë, strengthe, and right, / Tho fourë ben vertuës principal," as indicating a major part of the poem's advice. However, to my knowledge, no one has called attention to the structural plan whereby these four provide the basic framework for the poem.

Citations from *The Regement* in my text are to the edition by F. J. Furnivall, EETS, ES, LXXII (London, 1897).

Off magnanimite now wole I trete,
þat is to seyn, strong herte or grete corage,
Whiche in knyghthode haþ stablisshed hir sete.
Ye, gracious Prince, of blode and of lynage
Descendid ben, to haue it in vsage;
. . . .
He þat is strong of corage and of herte,—
Yf he lordschipës haue, or grete richesse,
Or þat fortunës stynge hym ouerthwerte,—
Is alwey on in welthe and in distresse;
He, lucre and los, weyeth in euenesse;
  He settiþ litel by good temperel;
  How þe worlde schape, he takiþ it ay wel.

Much in the passage has relevance to the thematic ideas found in *Magnyfycence:* the attitude *de contemptu mundi* advocated even for a king in the final lines is germane to that problem about the play, to be considered in the next chapter; the rôle of Fortune in a king's "ouerthwerte" parallels a similar emphasis at that point in the play (though certainly this is commonplace enough in medieval literature); the repeated stressing of "grete richesse," "welthe," and "lucre" not only suggests the prominence accorded such matters in the prosperity half of the play but provides a background in Hoccleve's own work for his later fuller development of true princely liberality. However, more significant than all of these, because inclusive of them all, is the basic definition of Magnanimity (or Fortitude, or sometimes Magnificence) as that strength of heart which enables a king to weigh "in euenesse" both "lucre and los," which helps him to be "alwey on" whether "in welthe" or "in distresse," whether he has lordship and "grete richesse" or is overthrown by fortune into adversity. A

83

closer study of the controlling pattern of ideas in *The Regement of Prynces* suggests, then, that the poem has even more striking affinities with *Magnyfycence* than Ramsay has suggested, the views on prodigality in the poem not only paralleling those in the play but being subsumed within a larger design just as scenes of prodigality within the play are limited to the early stages of prosperity where they are relevant, while the fuller sweep of the theme turns the play's action toward dramatizing other ethical problems also subordinate to the more inclusive design.

A full century earlier than Skelton's morality, *The Regement* bears somehow the aura of medievalism about its treatment of the virtue. Though not clerical and though related only as distant cousins to passages like those noted from manuals of religious instruction, its discourse upon the cardinal virtue differs little from them. The renewed humanistic interest in Cicero's *De officiis* itself, however, led to works in the sixteenth century which re-expressed the classical treatment of Fortitude. Whittinton's translation, with its marginal gloss to the prosperity-adversity motif, has already been mentioned; and it was soon followed by translations by Nicholas Grimald and others. More significant to the purposes of this study, courtiers like La Primaudaye and Lodowick Bryskett refracted the Ciceronian ideal of Fortitude through the prism of a humanistic viewpoint to produce such passages as this from Bryskett:

> The mind must be so disposed & armed against fortune, be she froward or fauorable, it may stand always inuincible against all misfortunes and aduersities, and yet not raise it selfe for prosperous successes. For it is as true a token of a base mind to be proud & insolent in prosperitie, as to be daunted and faint-hearted in aduersitie and affliction.... For who so is armed with

true fortitude, outward things whatsoeuer they be, neither giue nor take ought from them. But they that cannot temper themselues in prosperitie, nor beare aduersitie stoutly, make it apparant that fortune mastreth them.[20]

Similarly La Primaudaye affirms that "All mindes are not resolute and constant enough from slipping beside themselues, and beyond the limits of reason, neither in great prosperity, which puffeth and lifteth vp mens harts, especially theirs that are base by nature, nor yet in vnloked for aduersity, which through the heauie burthen thereof oftentimes astonisheth and amazeth them that are thought to be best setled and assured."[21] Consequently, he charges, in another place, "it is our dutie to keep our selues moderate, constant, and vpright, both in prosperitie and in aduersitie, which is the propertie of true magnanimitie and greatnes of courage. Let vs not lift vp our selues aboue measure for any temporall felicitie, nor be too much discouraged bicause we are visited with aduersitie" (p. 349).

Views like these, and others akin to them throughout sixteen centuries of reiteration and evolution, correspond with striking fidelity to the full range of ideas dramatized in *Magnyfycence*. Furthermore, *both* conflicts of the conventional morality structure that Skelton chose as a dramatic vehicle serve in transmuting ideas into action, the first conflict embodying the temptations of prosperity and the second, those of adversity. Indeed, the very opening lines of the play ("Al thyng ys contryuyd by mannys Reason,—/The world, enuyronnyd of Hygh and Low Estate") establish this pattern of alternate conditions through which the action is to move. With the homely imagery of folk analogy,

20. *A Discovrse of Civill Life* (London, 1606), pp. 216-17.
21. *The French Academie*, trans. T. B[owes] (London, 1586), p. 339.

the prologue cautions once more that just as "experyence trewe and playne" shows that

> ... after a drought there fallyth a showre of rayne,
> And after a hete oft cometh a stormy colde,—
> A man may haue Welth, but not as he wolde,
> Ay to contynewe and styll to endure.
>
> (ll. 11-15)

Both these didactic assertions appear in the opening soliloquy by Felycyte, which serves as a prologue to the play, and thus foreshadow the full scope of the intended action, including the often neglected second conflict as well as the first. To ignore such explicit indications of Skelton's design is to risk misreading the play by becoming involved in the first sequence of action before understanding its subordinate place within this larger perspective provided at the outset.

The morality drama proper begins with the appearance of Lyberte (or Will), who engages Felycyte (or Prosperity) in a *débat* whose heated verbal exchange serves effectively as a median between the expository moralizing of the prologue and the allegorized action soon to follow. Felycyte insists that "Lyberte be lynkyd with the chayne of Continence" since "Lyberte makyth many a man blynde; / By Lyberte is done many a great excesse; / Lyberte at large wyll oft wax reklesse" (ll. 44, 52-54). But in retort his opponent challenges:

> ... howe can ye proue that there is Felycyte,
> And you haue not your owne fre Lyberte,
>> To sporte at your pleasure, to ryn, and to ryde?
>> Where Lyberte is absent, set Welthe asyde!
>
> (ll. 77-80)

The threatening discord of this conflict is checked, temporarily at least, by the entrance of Measure, who, invoking Horace as his authority rather than Aristotle, mediates with the advice that

> With euery condycyon Measure must be sought.
> Welthe without Measure wolde bere hymselfe to bolde;
>   Lyberte without Measure proue a thynge of nought.
> (ll. 115-17)

The puzzling allusion to Horace will need further investigation later, but of more concern at the moment is the similarity of this advice to that repeatedly advanced in the passages on Fortitude cited earlier.

When Magnyfycence himself enters at this point, he too affirms the same principle when he instructs the disputants:

> Welthe with Lyberte, with me bothe dwell ye shall,
>   To the gydynge of my Measure you bothe commyttynge;
> That Measure be mayster, vs semeth it is syttynge.
> . . . .
> For by Measure I warne you we thynke to be gydyd;
>   Wherin it is necessary my pleasure you knowe:
> Measure and I wyll neuer be deuydyd,
>   For no dyscorde that any man can sawe;
>   For Measure is a meane, nother to hy nor to lawe,
>   In whose attemperaunce I haue suche delyght,
>   That Measure shall neuer departe from my syght.
> (ll. 174-76; 184-90)

Having so pledged himself (as La Primaudaye puts it) not to "lift vp our selues aboue measure for any temporall felicitie," the king confirms the intention by the allegorical act of putting Lyberte under the supervision of Measure while he consorts with his Felycyte.

Animating such clearly allegorical maneuvers is Skelton's talent in bringing to the morality, as he brought to the dream allegory of *The Bowge of Courte,* those strokes of individual personality that impart life to otherwise stiff conceptual beings. In *Magnyfycence,* as Maurice Pollet has recently reminded us, the character of Measure (whom the king from the first calls "my frende" [l. 165]) is given the manner and bearing of a statesman-like advisor at court while the four vices soon to dominate the action are drawn as court flatterers and intriguers.[22] In this light one of Cicero's often-cited passages from his discussion of Fortitude during prosperity and adversity provides an enlightening analogue to the pattern of action the dramatist develops here and throughout the remainder of the first, or prosperity, cycle: "In tyme of moste prosperyte we must chefely use the counsayle of our frendes, and we must gyue to them more authoritie than we dyd before. And in the same tymes we must be wyse and ware that we open not our eares to flatterers, nor suffre our selfe to be flattered, wherin decepcion is lyghtly founde. For we iudge our selfe such maner of men that we maye of ryght be praysed, wherof ryseth innumerable offenses whan men proude in their owne opinyon be shamfully had in derisyon, and be tossed in most errours."[23]

Skelton draws upon this motif ready at hand within the tradition of Fortitude (though not necessarily from the *De officiis* itself) in order to create a satisfying, motivated dramatic action that can carry his tempted king to the prodi-

22. *John Skelton (c. 1460-1529), Contribution à l'Histoire de la Prérenaissance Anglaise* ("Études Anglaises," IX [Paris, 1962], pp. 120-24.
23. *De officiis,* i. 26. 91, translated by Skelton's friend, Robert Whittinton (as cited in note 6 above), F1^v-F2^r.

gality, pride, and insolence which that same tradition taught to be the vicious extremes prosperity could induce. Magnyfycence, having "use[d] the counsayle of [his] frende," Measure, and having given him that "more authoritie" Cicero recommends, is immediately to be faced with the flatterers he should avoid. No sooner does Measure ironically proclaim,

> There is no flaterer nor losyll so lyther,
> This lynkyd chayne of loue that can vnbynde,
>
> (ll. 200-1)

than Fansy insinuates his way into the Prince's confidence through a forged letter from Cyrcumspeccyon (or Reason) and immediately tempts the king into prodigality by the grossest sycophancy:

> FAN. And in dede, Syr, I hear men talke,—
> By the way as I ryde and walke,—
> Say howe you excede in Noblenesse,
> If you had with you Largesse.
> MAGN. And say they so in very dede?
> FAN. With ye, Syr, so God me spede.
>
> (ll. 374-79)

In his wake come the courtier-vices with their self-proclaimed talents at court fawning and duplicity:

> CLOKED COLUSYON. From that lorde to that lorde
>   I rode and I ran,
> And flatered them with fables fayre before theyr face,
>   And tolde all the Myschyef I coude behynde theyr
>   backe.
>
> (ll. 716-18)

COUNTERFET COUNTENANCE.
        I set not by hym a fly
        That can not counterfet a lye,
        Swere, and stare, and byde therby,
        And countenaunce it clenly,
        And defende it manerly.
                          (ll. 412-16)
CRAFTY CONUEYAUNCE. Full moche Flatery and Falsehode
   I hyde.
                              (l. 1358)

These parasites find an easy outlet for such talents in manipulating a king who has mistaken his fantasy for his reason. Progressively, they induce him to expell his responsible advisor, to devote himself to foolish pleasures, and to turn more and more authority over to themselves. Not long after Fansy's opening fraud, he is able to initiate both of the first two objectives. He encounters the dandy, Courtly Abusyon, who has just revealed to the audience his frivolous nature; and the two greet each other with the following news:

   FANSY. What! whom haue we here, Jenkyn Joly? Nowe welcom, by the God holy!
      COURTLY ABUSYON. What! Fansy, my frende! howe doste thou fare?
   . . . .
   But nowe what tydynges can you tell? let se.
      FAN. Mary, I am come for the.
      COU. AB.   For me?
      FAN. Ye, for the, so I say.
      COU. AB. Howe so? tell me, I the pray.
      FAN. Why, harde thou not of the fray

That fell amonge vs this same day?
COU. AB. No, mary; not yet.
FAN. What the deuyll! neuer a whyt?
COU. AB. No, by the masse; what! sholde I swere?
FAN. In faythe, Lyberte is nowe a lusty spere.
COU. AB. Why, vnder whom was he abydynge?
FAN. Mary, Mesure had hym a whyle in gydynge,
Tyll, as the deuyll wolde, they fell a chydynge
With Crafty Conuayaunce.
COU. AB. Ye, dyd they so?
FAN. Ye, by Goddes sacrament; and with other mo.
COU. AB. What! neded that, in the dyuyls date?
FAN. Yes, yes; he fell with me also at debate.
COU. AB. With the also? what! he playeth the state?
FAN. Ye; but I bade hym pyke out of the gate;
By Goddes body, so dyd I.
COU. AB. By the masse, well done and boldely.
FAN. Holde thy pease! Measure shall frome vs
walke.
COU. AB. Why, is he crossed than with a chalke?
FAN. Crossed? ye, checked out of Consayte.
COU. AB. Howe so?
FAN. By God, by a praty slyght,
As here after thou shalte knowe more.
But I must tary here; go thou before.
(ll. 919-21, 929-55)

Giving his companion the alias of Lusty Pleasure (l. 965), Fansy returns to court and soon gains supervision over Felycyte (Prosperity) when Magnyfycence gives the task to him and the newly-released Lyberte in spite of the objections of their new charge that "Lyberte without rule is not worth a strawe" (l. 1378), "It is good yet that Lyberte be ruled by Reason" (l. 1387), "where is no Mesure, how may Worshyp endure?" (l. 1408). The protests are fruitless as the king listens rather to the parasitic flattery that "All that ye say, Syr, is Reason and Skyll" (l. 1381).

The matter settled, Magnyfycence turns his attention more fully to the pleasures being provided by the vices. Sending Fansy and Lyberte off with their new responsibility, he instructs them:

> MAGN. Well, get you hens than and sende me some
> other.
> FAN. Whom? Lusty Pleasure, or mery Consayte?
> MAGN. Nay, fyrst Lusty Pleasure is my desyre to
> haue;
> And let the other another time awayte;
> Howe be it, that fonde felowe is a mery knaue.
> But loke that ye occupye the auctoryte that I you gaue.
> (ll. 1451-56)

Courtly Abusyon soon appears, obsequiously "doynge reuerence and courtesy," and undertakes to divert him with extravagances of speech, manner, and dress; "to aqueynte [him] with Carnall Delectacyon"; and to teach him the art of arrogant abuse of those who displease him (scene 24). But the ultimate degeneracy is dramatized in a later scene with Foly—or "mery Consayte" as he is known to the king, who has already acknowledged, "That fonde felowe is a mery knaue." In contrast to the debauches of Courtly Abusyon, which are ludicrous excesses of very human conduct, the entertainment with which Foly enthralls Magnyfycence up to the moment of his downfall is one of sheer idiotic gibberish, all evidences of human reason gone.

Meanwhile, the plot to isolate the monarch from his more responsible advisors has reached its culmination.

Cloked Colusyon, pretending to Measure that he will seek reinstatement for him, actually betrays him into an even more violent rejection by the king (scene 25), who has ably learned the art of insolent vituperation from Courtly Abusyon. Emboldened by the success of his deceit, Cloked Colusyon bids for absolute authority for himself and his cronies. His advice is:

> Syr, of my counsayle this shall be the grounde:
> To chose out ii., iii., of suche as you loue best,
> And let all your Fansyes vpon them rest.
> Spare for no cost to gyue them pounde and peny;
> Better to make iii. ryche than for to make many.
> Gyue them more than ynoughe, and let them not lacke;
> And as for all other, let them trusse and packe
> Plucke from an hundred, and gyue it to thre;
> Let neyther patent scape them nor fee;
> And where soeuer you wyll fall to a rekenynge,
> Those thre wyll be redy euen at your bekenynge;
> For them shall you haue at Lyberte to lowte.
> Let them haue all, and the other go without;
> Thus Ioy without Mesure you shall haue.
> (ll. 1768-81)

The king readily accepts the proposal, giving the courtier-vices full control, even over the previously favored Fansy and Lyberte (ll. 1782ff).

Thus isolated, distracted, and excessively admired, Magnyfycence has reached that point of self-esteem of which Cicero warns ("we iudge our selfe such maner of men that we maye of ryght be praysed"). During a prolonged Herodian soliloquy he boasts, "I am prynce perlesse, prouyd of porte"; elevates himself above history's mightiest monarchs, who "may not be comparyd vnto me. / I am the dyamounde dowtlesse of dygnyte. / Surely it is I that all may saue and spyll, / No man so hardy to worke agaynst my Wyll"; and predicts that he can "folowe in Felycyte without reuersse; / I drede no daunger; I dawnce all in delyte: / My name is Magnyfycence, man most of myght" (ll. 1471, 1476-79, 1491-93). When a sycophant admires, "Nowe Jesu preserue you, Syr, prynce most of might!" (l. 1796), he brags, "Thus, I say, I am enuyronned with Solace; / I dred no dyntes of fatall Desteny" (ll. 1797-98). Disaster cannot be—and is not—far away.

Precisely such consequences as these—the dismissal of responsible advisors, the addiction to frivolous pleasures, the exclusive reliance upon parasites, and the proud and arrogant denial of human finitude—all these were part of the picture that sixteenth-century instructors of princes evoked to expand upon Cicero's warning against the loss of Fortitude "in tyme of most prosperyte." For example, La Primaudaye goes on to say, almost as an exact parallel to Skelton's dramatic action, that all the efforts of sycophants at such times are "to propound vnto vs occasions & meanes to enioy delights and pleasures, and to shew our selues to be proud and arrogant, during the time of our prosperitie: to the end we should put good men farre from vs, and reserue to them onely [i.e., the sycophants] that authority wherin they are setled. Whereas on the contrarie side our true friends would lead vs backe to consider the inconstancie of humane things, to the ende that we abuse not our felicitie."[24]

Skelton structured his morality, it would appear then, primarily upon the prosperity-adversity pattern associated with the cardinal virtue of Fortitude (or Magnificence) and supplemented each half of this design with subsidiary

24. *The French Academie,* p. 341.

motifs also associated with the same virtue. Thus, while the prologue adumbrates the full sweep of action—upward beyond measure in prosperity and then downward into like immoderation during adversity—the opening conflict of virtues and vices that follows it carries the protagonist to those extremes of conduct which prosperity was said to encourage. By developing this sequence of events in terms of characters and episodes suggested by those warnings against flatterers, intrigues, and debilitating pleasures which continued to accrue to the basic definition of Fortitude from the time of Cicero on up through the sixteenth century, Skelton was able not only to achieve a reasonably motivated development of character and events beyond the usual static portrayals typical of the medieval morality but, more significantly, to dramatize graphically those very conditions against which he would warn his own monarch during his "tyme of most prosperyte." Thus, in the opening half of the play, many of the ideas and incidents which have led to speculation that they are founded upon specific events and personalities at Henry's court and to assumptions of a truncated and radically modified Aristotelian theme can be seen instead to be part of a tradition sufficiently rich to account for all the details.

Similarly, the last half of the play, which has been ignored by modern readers as an artistic *non sequitur,* continues by extension this same design. In fact, so smooth is the transition and so organic the development from one phase to the other that even to define "the last half of the play," much less to conceive of it as irrelevant to the opening scenes, is to misconstrue both the dramatist's design and that of the tradition he follows.

In the *De officiis,* for example, the passage on the dangers of prosperous intemperance, which provided Skelton with his dramatic action in the early scenes, leads to the warning (and the remedy) that "men that be in prosperyte, beyng as vnbrydled and truste to moche of them selfe, must be brought in to a compace of reason and lernyng, to thentent they may se the fragylite of transytory thynges, and dyuers chaunge of fortune."[25] The trials of adversity, also to be borne with Fortitude, provide this "compace of reason and lernynge." Thus, in *Magnyfycence* the sudden advent of disaster at the moment of the king's greatest folly and ultimate presumption is depicted as both the inevitable consequence of, and the necessary remedy for, his lack of Fortitude in prosperity.

The first, or retributive, function is performed by the allegorical figure of Aduersyte, who enters upon Fansy's exclamation to Magnyfycence that the flatterers have "brought vs in Aduersyte, / And had robbyd you quyte from all Felycyte" (ll. 1863-64). The first words of this terrible figure emphasize his mission and its divine origin: "I am Aduersyte, that for thy mysdede / From God am sent to quyte the thy mede" (ll. 1876-77). Repeatedly stressing that he is "The Stroke of God" and "Goddys Preposytour," he instructs the audience directly that his punishment of Magnyfycence is in proportion to the king's excesses in prosperity:

> I plucke downe kynge, prynce, lorde, and knyght;
> I rushe at them rughly and make them ly full lowe;
> And in theyr moste truste I make them ouerthrowe.
> Thys losyll was a lorde and lyuyd at his lust;
> And nowe lyke a lurden he lyeth in the duste.
> He knewe not hymselfe, his harte was so hye;
> Nowe is there no man that wyll set by hym a flye.

25. I. 26. 90. Whittinton's translation, E8^v-F1^r.

He was wonte to boste, brage, and to brace;
Nowe dare he not for shame loke one in the face.
All worldly Welth for hym to lytell was;
Nowe hath he ryght nought, naked as an asse.
Somtyme without Measure he trusted in golde;
And now without Measure he shal haue hunger and colde.
. . . .

Wherfore of Aduersyte loke ye be ware;
For when I come, comyth Sorowe and Care;
For I stryke lordys of realmes and landys
That rule not by Mesure that they haue in theyr handys.
(ll. 1883-95, 1936-39)

While Aduersyte's attitude toward the king is one of retribution (all edification being directed to those beyond the play), he is followed by Pouerte, whose first concern is to teach the king himself so that he "may se the fragylite of transytory thynges, and dyuers chaunge of fortune." When Magnyfycence recalls in perplexity that he "wenyd ones neuer to haue knowen of Care," his mentor warns: "Lo, suche is this worlde! I fynde in wryt, / In Welth to beware; and that is Wyt" (ll. 1973-75). Such advice he expounds at length, before concluding:

Syr, remembre the tourne of Fortunes whele,
That wantonly can wynke, and wynche with her hele.
Nowe she wyll laughe; forthwith she wyll frowne;
Sodenly set vp and sodenly pluckyd downe;
She dawnsyth varyaunce with mutabylyte,
Nowe all in Welth, forthwith in Pouerte;
In her promyse there is no sykernesse;
All her Delyte is set in Doublenesse.
(ll. 2022-29)

This latter passage, even when the broad conventionality of the wheel of fortune is discounted, is striking in two ways. Pouerte's having said it as the culmination of an allegorical sequence whereby an intemperately prosperous ruler has been brought into adversity so that he can learn of this world's mutability provides a dramatization of the *De officiis* passage. But, even beyond this indication of continuing fidelity to the Fortitude tradition, both form and content of the speech contribute to the unifying design Skelton has woven into the play's language. Here, near dead center, as the play pivots to shift emphasis from the temptations of prosperity to those of adversity, occurs a passage whose echoes of sound and sense resonate with those heard in balanced passages in prologue and epilogue. Already noticed is the play's first speech, which notes that in this life wealth gives way to poverty just as drought turns to rain and as heat yields to cold. There, the implications foreshadow the play's full scope before the first condition of wealth is dramatized. Here, at mid-play, as this condition leads into its counterpart, the same wisdom is heard in balanced phrases that echo the earlier passage and, like it, reflect the structural rhythm of the whole play. Finally, when the second condition has run its course, the epilogue is to expand the note into a crescendo which, if monotonously sustained, is at least clearly indicative of the poet's design. I cite only portions:

A myrrour incleryd is this interlude,
  This lyfe inconstant for to beholde and se:
Sodenly auaunsyd, and sodenly subdude;
  Sodenly Ryches, and sodenly Pouerte;
    Sodenly Comfort, and sodenly Aduersyte;
      Sodenly thus Fortune can bothe smyle and frowne,
      Sodenly set vp, and sodenly cast downe.

To day fayre wether, to morowe a stormy rage;
To day hote, to morowe outragyous colde;
To day a yoman, to morowe made of page;
To day in surety, to morowe bought and solde;
To day maysterfest, to morowe he hath no holde;
To day a man, to morowe he lyeth in the duste:
Thus in this worlde there is no erthly truste.

(ll. 2519-25, 2540-46)

The same idea, the same rhythm, even the same figures unite the three passages to bring into repeated perspective at crucial intervals the larger structural-thematic design upon which the drama is conceived.

But, to return to Pouerte's role as divine mentor to the immoderate king, it must be emphasized that his advice goes beyond just showing Magnyfycence "the fragylite of transytory thynges" on which he had built his prosperous presumption. This advice shifts the drama's emphasis onto the new condition of adversity. However, while adversity may by its very nature be therapeutic to some degree, it too requires a concomitant Fortitude lest its demands on human character destroy the sufferer. Thus, Pouerte encourages an attitude of moderate acceptance: "All that God sendeth, take it in gre" (l. 1979). Magnyfycence, however, is as passionately excessive in his grief as he was in his joy and thrashes about in remorse and self-pity, while Pouerte urges repeatedly,

... leue all this rage,
And pray to God your sorowes to asswage.
It is Foly to grudge agaynst his vysytacyon.
With harte contryte make your supplycacyon

> Vnto your Maker, that made bothe you and me;
> And whan it pleaseth God, better may be.
>
> (ll. 1988-93)
>
> Remembre you better, Syr; beware what ye say,
> For drede ye dysplease the hygh Deyte.
> Put your Wyll to His wyll, for surely it is He
> That may restore you agayne to Felycyte,
> And brynge you agayne out of Aduersyte.
> Therefore Pouerte loke pacyently ye take. . . .
>
> (ll. 1995-2000)
>
> Ye, Syr, yesterday wyll not be callyd agayne.
> But yet, Syr, nowe in this case
> Take it mekely, and thanke God of his grace;
>
> . . . .
>
> It is Foly agaynst God for to plete.
>
> (ll. 2031-35)

The allusions to Foly and Wyll as well as the balancing of Felycyte against Aduersyte serve to parallel the present situation and conduct with that dramatized earlier; the recommendations of patient acceptance of misfortune and heavenly rebuke emphasize the kind of moderation appropriate to adversity just as moderation of a different sort was appropriate to prosperity. As was the case in the earlier sequence, these counsels of moderation in adversity are not firmly heeded; and the protagonist progressively deteriorates in the following scenes until, as earlier, he lends his ear to advisors (Dyspare and Myschefe) whose diabolically extreme suggestions lead him again to the brink of disaster, from which this time he is rescued.

Before undertaking a more detailed study of these scenes which carry the action toward the second morality conflict, however, it is necessary to return to the development of the cardinal virtues throughout the centuries before Skelton. Such a closer re-examination is required lest superficial similarities between the tradition and the morality play at this point be taken as more real than they are. Specifically, the problem is one of not confusing the Stoic words and ideas out of which the cardinal virtue tradition grew with the Christian concepts that had long since modified, replaced, or grown up alongside them.

For instance, complementing his expansive treatment of Fortitude during prosperity, Cicero says of adversity that "fortis vero animi et constantis est non perturbari in rebus asperis nec tumultuantem de gradu deici, ut dicitur, sed praesenti animo uti et consilio nec a ratione discedere" (*De officiis* i. 23. 80). In a general sense, of course, this can be said to be just what Skelton's king fails to do "in rebus asperis." Actually, however, Cicero's concern, as his fuller discussions reveal, is for coolheadedness in times of military and civil danger. This practical republican emphasis was to appeal to the humanistic instructors of renaissance princes, but it finds no place at all in Skelton's play.

However, the process of Christian adaptation which modified the whole Stoic ethic in so many respects had altered the nature of this portion of it long before Skelton's age so that it admonished a humbly patient acceptance of personal adversity that might prevent man from abject despair and even suicide, the course nearly followed by Magnyfycence. Evidences of this Christian adaptation are present as early as the imitative *De officiis ministrorum* (*ca.* 391) of St. Ambrose. As noticed earlier, Ambrose follows Cicero closely, entitling one chapter, "Servandam ut in prosperis, ita et in adversis mentis aequalitatem"; beginning it with the familiar admonition, "Ea est etiam quae dicitur vacuitas animi ab angoribus; ut neque in doloribus molliores simus, neque in prosperis elatiores," and affirming one more time that "verum quia fortitudo non solum secundis rebus, sed etiam adversis probatur." But, in expanding the principle in detail, he emphasizes an adversity of personal misfortune and a patient bearing of it: "Quod cum ita affectus animo fueris, necesse est illud honestum ac decorum praeponendum putes, illique mentem ita intendas tuam, ut quidquid acciderit quo frangi animi solent, aut patrimonii amissio, aut honoris imminutio, aut obstrectatio infidelium, quasi superior non sentias."[26] Thus, his *exempla* of conduct in adversity are Job and the suffering Christ, just as Magnyfycence is reminded in his trials that he should remember how Christ "suffered moche for your sake" (l. 2001).

Julianus Pomerius' *De vita contemplativa* (*ca.* 500), however, seems to provide the earliest extant work in which Fortitude is explicitly held up as the *remedium* against complete despair, though actually behind Pomerius' passage lies a more famous one by St. Augustine. The Augustinian statement should be noted first, although it does not appear strictly in the context of a discussion of the cardinal virtues. In the opening book of *De civitate Dei,* Augustine finds occasion to prove the superiority of Christian sufferance to the pagan Roman custom of suicide as the honorable man's last defiance of worldly adversity. The title of one chapter during this section affirms, "Quod numquam possit mors voluntaria ad magnitudinem animi pertinere" and goes on to insist that "ne ipsa quidem animi magnitudo recte nominatur, ubi quisque non valendo tolerare vel quaeque aspera vel aliena peccata se ipse interemerit. Magis enim mens infirma deprehenditur, quae ferre non potest vel duram sui coporis servitutem vel stultam vulgi opinio-

26. I. 37. 185, i. 41. 199, i. 36. 181 (*PL*, XVI, 84, 89, 82).

nem, maiorque animus merito dicendus est, qui vitam aerumnosam magis potest ferre quam fugere."[27]

When Pomerius came to write his treatise, he devoted his climactic third book to giving an affirmative answer to a query as to whether there is any truth in the four virtues of pagan philosophy. Cicero is his guide in analyzing the four, so one reads such familiar assertions as, "Animi fortitudo ea debet intelligi quae non solum diversis pulsata molestiis inconcussa permaneat, sed etiam nullis voluptatum illecebris resoluta succumbat."[28] Augustine is at the same time his spiritual guide, so Pomerius affirms that in reality the God of Christianity "fortitudo nostra est, quia ita nos contra omnia vitia invicta protectione corroborat, ut animum nostrum nec blanda dissolvant, nec adversa dejiciant." Thus, he seems to be following Augustine when he conceives of the Christian's Fortitude as a defense against that "cowardice of despair" (*ignavia desperandi*) which leads to suicide in adversity: ". . . modo absit ignavia, ne nos id desperemus posse quod possumus; absit praesumptio vitiosa, ne nobis hoc quod per Dei gratiam possumus ascribamus. Quia siva de munere Dei, quo fortes efficimur, desperemus; sive nos de nostra possibilitate jactemus, idonei ad resistendum vitiis esse non possumus. Et utique animi fortitudo tam desperandi ignaviam debet executere quam jactantiae contraire."[29]

This early in the history of Christian adaptations of the

[27] I. 22. Edited by B. Dombart (Leipzig, 1877), I, 36.
[28] *De vita contemplativa*, iii. 20 (*PL*, LIX, 503).
[29] *Ibid.*, pp. 504-5. The Ciceronian and the Augustinian bases for Pomerius' work are indicated, respectively, in M. L. W. Laistner, "The Influence during the Middle Ages of the Treatise *De vita contemplativa* and Its Surviving Manuscripts," *Miscellanea Giovanni Mercati*, II (Vatican, 1946), 345; and in Sister Mary Josephine Suelzer's introduction to her translation of the treatise in *Ancient Christian Writers*, IV, ed. Johannes Quasten and Joseph C. Plumpe (Westminster, Md., 1947), p. 11.

Stoic virtues appears exactly the balance of extremes faced by Skelton's hero. The temptation to presumption and boasting in prosperity merely continues the *De officiis* emphasis upon these, but the concern with despair in adversity is a Christian one destined to become increasingly influential until Skelton chose the motif as the means of dramatizing the second conflict of his morality.

Of course, it should again be noted that the dramatist need not by any means have had the *De vita contemplativa* itself in mind, although the treatise did enjoy "an immense vogue right down to the sixteenth century" as evidenced by well over a hundred extant manuscripts as well as numerous entries in medieval library catalogues.[30] What is significant is not the treatise itself but the breadth of the stream generated by it. Its influence during the Carolingian revival of learning reached the exceptional proportions of gaining it an authoritativeness approaching that of the leading Latin fathers themselves.[31] Excerpts from it appear in the writings of the outstanding scholars of the period. For example, in the *De vitiis et virtutibus et de ordine poenitentium* by Halitgar, Bishop of Cambrai, the discussion of Fortitude consists of the statements by Pomerius rendered almost literally; and Hrabanus Maurus was content in turn to borrow Halitgar's redaction for his *De vitiis et virtutibus et peccatorum satisfactione.*[32]

30. Laistner, "Influence," *Miscellanea,* pp. 351-56, 358 (the essay was reprinted in *The Intellectual Heritage of the Early Middle Ages: Selected Essays by M. L. W. Laistner,* ed. Chester G. Starr [Ithaca, N. Y., 1957], where the pertinent references occur on pp. 48-53, 55-56). See also Laistner's review of E. R. Curtius, *Europäische Literatur und lateinisches Mittelalter* (Bern, 1948) in *Speculum,* XXIV (1949), 263 (reprinted in *The Intellectual Heritage,* p. 89).

31. Laistner, "Influence," *Miscellanea,* pp. 349-50 (pp. 46-48 in *The Intellectual Heritage*).

32. The passage in Halitgar's work may be found in *PL,* CV, 675 and Hrabanus' version in *PL,* CXII, 1337-38. It has been claimed that

Less dependent on Pomerius for its wording but still clearly in the tradition that had come to oppose Fortitude as the shield against despair in adversity is another passage from the writings of Hrabanus. Versifying the four cardinal virtues, he has one couplet headed *De fortitudine patientiae*, which reads:

> Fortiter adversa virtus patientia suffert,
> Victrix confidens tristia cuncta fugat.
> (*PL*, CXII, 1632)

The key word is *tristia* (or *tristitia*), one of the seven deadly sins according to Gregory the Great, later to be subsumed by the term *acedia* or *accidia*.[33] Designating that soul-weariness which leads man to self-destruction, *tristitia* is the parallel of Pomerius' *ignavia desperandi* and, like it, is overcome by the cardinal virtue of Fortitude. The terminology changes, but the concept remains.

By the time of the scholastic synthesis, *tristitia* had become the conventionally accepted theological term for that condition which leads to suicide unless checked by Fortitude. The writings of both Albert the Great and St. Thomas Aquinas provide cases in point. Treating Fortitude in his *Ethicorum libros x,* for instance, Albert entitles one chapter, "De comparatione fortitudinis ad extrema sua," and, after citing the example of Dido's suicide, says, "Alii autem interficiunt seipsos, ne diu sustineant aliquid aliud triste. Qui omnes licet aggrediantur arduissima et sustineant difficillima, sicut mortem, tamen non fortes, sed molles et

---

Hrabanus knew the *De vita contemplativa* first hand and was influenced by it in writing his *De anima* (see Max Manitius, *Geschichte der Lateinischen Literatur des Mittelalters* [Munich, 1911], I, 293); but Laistner feels that such was not necessarily the case ("Influence," *Miscellanea*, p. 351, or *The Intellectual Heritage*, pp. 47-48).

33. For a fuller treatment of this development, see Morton W. Bloomfield, *The Seven Deadly Sins* (East Lansing, Mich., 1952), pp. 69-77, 356.

timidi sunt: quia difficillima sustinent, ut tristitiam evadant: et hoc dejecti et vilis et imbecillis animi est."[34]

St. Thomas' handling of the question in the *Summa theologica* is especially interesting because it reveals rather clearly the grafting of Christian ideas and terminology upon the body of Ciceronian ethics. As noticed in the previous chapter, St. Thomas organizes his analysis about Cicero's four sub-virtues to Fortitude and divides these virtues into two categories—those conducive to aggressiveness (magnificence and magnanimity), and those conducive to endurance (patience and perseverance). When, under the second category, he comes to the point of giving Cicero's definition of patience, he introduces it by explaining that the virtue assures that "ne difficultate imminentium malorum animus frangatur per tristitiam" (II-II, Q128). The major portion of this clause is quite consistent with Cicero's Stoic expressions; but for the last phrase, of course, there is no basis in Cicero whatsoever. With the subtle modifications implicit in a thoroughly Christianized term, St. Thomas has oriented the whole passage in accordance with what had become the orthodox ethical position derived from the Augustinian-Pomerian tradition. Thus, when St. Thomas develops this sub-virtue to Fortitude more at large, he does so by a repetitive emphasis upon *tristitia* and by more explicit indications of its suicidal connotations:

> Dicendum quod . . . virtutes morales ordinantur ad bonum inquantum conservant bonum rationis contra impetus passionum. Inter alias autem passiones tristitia efficax est ad impediendum bonum rationis, secundum illud II *ad Cor.* VII: "Saeculi tristitia mortem operatur"; et *Eccli.* XXX: "Multos occidit tristitia, et non est utilitas

[34.] iii. 2. 5. *Opera omnia,* ed. Augustus Borgnet (Paris, 1891), VII, 242. See also iii. 2. 11 (*ibid.,* VII, 250-51).

in illa." Unde necesse est habere aliquam virtutem per quam bonum rationis conservetur contra tristitiam, ne scilicet ratio tristitiae succumbat. Hoc autem facit patientia. Unde Augustinus dicit in libro *De Patientia,* quod "patientia hominis ... est qua mala aequo animo toleramus," idest sine perturbatione tristitiae, "ne animo iniquo bona deseramus per quae ad meliora perveniamus" (II-II, Q136, a1).

St. Thomas, like Hrabanus, it might also be observed, assigns the function of resisting despair not just to Fortitude in general but to patience, one of its passive or enduring species. Through the centuries, even up to Milton's *Samson Agonistes,* this particular refinement was to become a major one.[35] When patience is urged upon Skelton's monarch in his torment (l. 2000), possibly the same orthodoxy is being reflected. There were, however, exceptions to this ramification. One twelfth-century florilegium, for example, cites "magnificentia in exercitu fortitudinis primipilana" as the combatant of "accidia uel ... tristicia huius seculi."[36] Chaucer's parson, on the other hand, seems at one point to invoke Fortitude itself and then again to recommend a species of it. Since his discussion is relevant in many other ways as well, I shall cite it in some detail.

Rehearsing the terrible manifestations of "this rotenherted synne of Accidie," the gentle parson dwells at length upon "wanhope, that is despeir of the mercy of God, that comth somtyme of to muche outrageous sorwe, and somtyme of to muche drede, ymaginynge that he hath doon so muche synne that it wol nat availlen hym, though he wolde re-

35. William O. Harris, "Despair and 'Patience as the Truest Fortitude' in *Samson Agonistes,*" *ELH*, XXX (1963), 107-15.
36. *Florilegium morale oxoniense, Ms. Bodl. 633: Prima pars, flores philosophorum,* ed. Ph. Delhaye, in *Analecta Mediaevalia Namurcensia,* V (Louvain, 1955), p. 98.

penten hym and forsake synne." As we shall see, both of these causes of ultimate despair—the "outrageous sorwe" (or *tristitia*) as well as the belief that one's sins exceed God's forgiveness—Skelton dramatizes as successive stages in the path Magnyfycence follows to the point of self-destruction. Chaucer's parson is particularly concerned about the latter, treating it at length and concluding with the exhortation, "Certes, ther is noon so horrible synne of man that it ne may in his lyf be destroyed by penitence, thurgh vertu of the passion and of the deeth of Crist. Allas! what nedeth man thanne to been despeired, sith that his mercy so redy is and large? Axe and have." Concerning the former, he says in his climactic passage on Accidia, "Thanne comth the synne of worldly sorwe, swich as is cleped *tristicia,* that sleeth man, as seith Seint Paul. For certes, swich sorwe werketh to the deeth of the soule and of the body also; for therof comth that a man is anoyed of his owene lif. Wherfore swich sorwe shorteth ful ofte the lif of man, er that his tyme be come by wey of kynde." Turning immediately to the *remedium,* he assures his listeners that

> Agayns this horrible synne of Accidie, and the branches of the same, ther is a vertu that is called *fortitudo* or strengthe, that is an affeccioun thurgh which a man despiseth anoyouse thinges. This vertu is so myghty and so vigerous that it dar withstonde myghtily and wisely kepen hymself fro perils that been wikked, and wrastle agayn the assautes of the devel. For it enhaunceth and enforceth the soule, right as Accidie abateth it and maketh it fieble. For this *fortitudo* may endure by long suffraunce the travailles that been covenable.
>
> This vertu hath manye speces; and the firste is cleped magnanimitee, that is to seyn, greet corage. For certes,

ther bihoveth greet corage agains Accidie, lest that it ne swolwe the soule by the synne of sorwe, or destroye it by wanhope.

Completing the list of "speces" (which seems to be an abbreviated amalgam of the lists given by Cicero and Macrobius), he cites "magnificence" as well as "seuretee" and "constaunce."[37]

In the productive centuries between Pomerius and Hrabanus on the one hand and Chaucer and Skelton on the other, this Christian adaptation of Fortitude and its subordinate virtues into a defense against despair and suicide had become increasingly widespread; and, while variations and modifications in bewildering array confront one at every turn, there remains a unity of general concept even when tangential developments occur and real origins are almost obliterated. An excellent example of the strength and consistency of this doctrine, even when the original confines of the cardinal virtue tradition that gave it birth had been transcended, is apparent throughout the evolution of the septenaries of vices, virtues, gifts of the Holy Spirit, beatitudes, pater noster petitions, etc. In fact, Chaucer's Fortitude, while its species as well as its opposition to despair reveal the unmistakable characteristics of the cardinal virtue tradition, is set in a foreign context of other *remedia* for the seven sins which derive from the septenaries and the manuals of religious instruction based upon them. A brief survey of a portion of the whole complex matter may clarify the situation somewhat, though it also runs the risk of oversimplification.

One of the most troublesome and controversial problems to occupy the debating theologians as the septenaries

---

37. *The Complete Works of Geoffrey Chaucer*, ed. Fred N. Robinson (2nd ed.; Boston, 1957), pp. 249-51.

evolved was that of the exact relationship between the cardinal virtues and the seven gifts. The question is far too complex and extensive to treat here,[38] but one aspect of it is especially relevant. While the two lists varied considerably (the gifts being Fortitude, Fear of God, Piety, Knowledge, Counsel, Understanding, and Wisdom; and the virtues being Fortitude, Temperance, Justice, Prudence, Faith, Hope, and Love), the one point of unmistakably congruent terminology was that of Fortitude. Those who argued the synonymity of the gifts and virtues sometimes cited this fact as support of their thesis. While this view that gifts and virtues were identical did not eventually triumph in church circles, the coincidence of terms at Fortitude seems to account for the fact that, as early as Hugh of St. Victor's pioneering alignment of gifts as *remedia* against the sins, the gift of Fortitude was arraigned in defense against "acedia seu tristitia,"[39] the traditional foe of the cardinal virtue. Followed by John of Salisbury, Alanus de

38. An exhaustive study of the matter, especially as it was debated during the twelfth and thirteenth centuries, can be found in Lottin, *Psychologie et Morale*, III, 329-456, and in such articles of his as "The Thomist Theory of the Gifts of the Holy Spirit in the Last Quarter of the Thirteenth Century," *Dominican Studies*, II (1949), 104-44, and "Le Traité d'Alain de Lille sur les Vertus, les Vices et les Dons du Saint-Esprit," *Mediaeval Studies*, XII (1950), 20-56. Also helpful are A. Gardiel, "Dons du Saint-Esprit," *Dictionnaire de Théologie Catholique*, ed. A. Vacant, et al., IV (1911), 1747-79; and Jean-François Bonnefoy, *Le Saint-Esprit et ses dons selon saint Bonaventure*, Vol. X of *Études de Philosophie Médiévale*, ed. Etienne Gilson (Paris, 1929), pp. 79-98. All of these I have relied upon heavily in deriving the oversimplified generalities of this paragraph.

39. *De quinque septenis seu septenariis*, i and iv (*PL*, CLXXV, 405 and 409), translated by Joachim Wach, "Hugo of St. Victor on Virtues and Vices," *Anglican Theological Review*, XXXI (1949), 25-33. See, also, the *De sacramentis*, ii. 13. 2 (*PL*, CLXXVI, 527) and *Expositio moralia in Abdiam* (*PL*, CLXXV, 403-4) as well as Lottin, *Psychologie et Morale*, III, 436n.

Insulis, St. Bonaventure, and many others,[40] regardless of their position in the gifts-virtues controversy, the alignment became probably the most stable of any of the remedial pairings. The influence and continuity of the cardinal virtue definitions in this related context is especially apparent when one reads the manuals of religious instruction that popularized the septenary. In his *Somme le Roi,* for instance, Frere Lorens organizes his discussion of the gift of Fortitude around Macrobius' species of the cardinal virtue (magnanimity, magnificence, etc.) and also turns to Pomerius' *De vita contemplativa* for Christian emphases.[41] It is not surprising, then, that Fortitude is said to be the only defense against *accidia,* which "ledeþ a man to þe ende" when he fails to obey God's penance. When, instead, such a man will "no þing suffre for impacience" and responds to deserved reproofs grudgingly and in anger, he eventually "falleþ in sorwe [*tristitia*] and is euele apaied of his self, and hateþ hymself and desireþ his owne deeþ" so that "þe deuel ȝyueþ hym a stroke of deeþ and put hym in wanhope and purchaseþ in deeþ and sleeþ hym."[42] As a closer study of the comparable portion of *Magnyfycence* will show,

40. John of Salisbury, *De septem septenis,* v (*PL,* CXCIX, 954); Alanus de Insulis, *De virtutibus et de vitiis et de donis Spiritus Sancti,* iii. 2, in Lottin, *Psychologie et Morale,* VI, 89; for St. Bonaventure, see Bonnefoy, *Le Saint-Esprit,* pp. 220-21. For others, see excerpts cited in Lottin, *Psychologie et Morale,* III, 349, 358.

41. A detailed analysis of Lorens' indebtedness to Pomerius may be found in Father John B. Dwyer, "The Tradition of Medieval Manuals of Instruction in the Poems of John Gower, with Special Reference to the Development of the Book of Virtues" (Ph.D. dissertation, University of North Carolina, 1950), pp. 269-71.

42. Quotations are from the Middle English translation of the *Somme le Roi,* edited by W. Nelson Francis as *The Book of Vices and Virtues,* EETS, OS, CCXVII (London, 1942), p. 29. See also Morris, ed., *The Ayenbite of Inwyt,* pp. 33-34, 163ff; and *Jacob's Well, Part I,* ed. Arthur Brandeis, EETS, OS, 115 (London, 1900), pp. 112-13, 287-90.

such a course of degeneration Skelton dramatizes for his beleaguered king.

This Christian version of Fortitude's rôle in adversity having become so widespread, it is only natural that the ethical instructors of the nobility during, and even beyond, Skelton's century made use of it as part of their advice. For instance, the hero of Jean Cartigny's allegory, *The Voyage of the Wandering Knight,* accepts the guidance of Dame Folly, who leads him to the Palace of Worldly Felicity, where he abandons himself to the pleasures of prosperity before he falls into a bog (much like Bunyan's Slough of Despond), where, as he relates, "such was my perplexity in this case that I fell in despair."[43] Lamenting frantically, he is rescued only by the sudden advent of "God's Grace" (as "Good Hope" rescues Magnyfycence) and undergoes a program of re-edification, including instruction in the four virtues, most especially Fortitude, "a virtue unto the which belongs a magnificent courage." "He that hath this virtue," he is reminded, "keeps himself constant in adversity and waxeth not proud in Prosperity" (p. 105). The particular temptation of adversity which will try his constancy is made explicitly clear: "Moreover such as extraordinarily and desperately dispatch themselves, as wretches weary of life, they do it not by Fortitude, but by the temptation of the devil, who is permitted by God's sufferance to tempt some even to the making away of themselves. Such people are weak-hearted and not valiant; for valiantness, which is Fortitude, is not named notable unless it be in lawful actions and deeds" (p. 106).

Others whose concern was to provide ethical instruction to the nobility seem to reflect the same tradition. In *The*

43. Trans. William Goodyear, ed. Dorothy Atkinson Evans (Seattle, 1951), p. 51.

French Academie, La Primaudaye insists that "if we consider apart the pernitious effects which issue from these two contraries [i.e., prosperity and adversity], when reason doth not guide and gouerne them, we shall find nothing but pride in the one, and ... oftentimes despaire in the other" (pp. 339-40). Concerning the latter, he sounds particularly Augustinian when he observes that suicide was "the common remedie of the Ancients in desperate cases," cites the instances of Cato, Brutus, and others, and concludes that "albeit these examples and infinite other like to these, are set foorth vnto vs by Historiographers, as testimonies of an excellent Magnanimitie, ... yet notwithstanding, no man that feareth God, and is willing to obey him, ought to forget himselfe so much, as to hasten forward the end of his daies for any occasion whatsoeuer" (pp. 290-93). Also, Spenser's Despair, whose temptation of the Red Crosse Knight is analogous to the one presented to Magnyfycence, is nearly successful because his victim, says H. S. V. Jones, lacks the cardinal virtue of Fortitude as Thomas Aquinas defines it.[44] To cite only one further example, Barnabe Barnes, following Cicero with even more fidelity than was usual among renaissance imitators, is nevertheless more Augustinian-Pomerian at one point in asserting that

> Them that in desperate causes as in respect of pouertie ... should kill or cast away themselues ... I cannot hold to be verely valiant; whereas it is the part of true valor [i.e., Fortitude] to beare in equall ballance of minde mischiefe, and prosperitie; a sure token of cowardize and idlenesse [*accidia*] also, to distrust, faint, or filthily to be deiected in troubles. Impacience ... opposeth it: such as are afraid to take paines and to be grieued

44. "The *Faerie Queene* and the Mediaeval Aristotelian Tradition," *JEGP*, XXV (1926), 290.

... are in this opposition: and such likewise as cannot bear honours and prosperitie with moderation (but become insolent without measure) are in as much fault or more.[45]

Such analogies as are discernible between a statement like this and the basic design and details of Skelton's morality result not because one is the progenitor of the other but because each derives from the same tradition of the Stoic-Christian virtue of Fortitude.

This motif of degeneracy into despair when one fails to adhere to the patience of Fortitude during adversity provides Skelton a pattern which he creatively expands into his second morality conflict just as the motifs long associated with the temptations of prosperity served as his model for the dramatic action that informs the first half of the play. At the outset of prosperity it was Measure, the counselor, who pronounced the wisdom of control to the king and so provided a doctrinal norm from which the falling off into the excessive vices of prosperity could develop, and against which this vicious course could be contrasted; similarly, Pouerte's admonitions now provide the fallen king a virtuous mode of conduct:

> Put your Wyll to His wyll, for surely it is He
> That may restore you agayne to Felycyte,
> And brynge you agayne out of Aduersyte.
> Therefore Pouerte loke pacyently ye take.
>
> (ll. 1997-2000)

The response of Magnyfycence to this wisdom of orthodoxy, however, creates the impression of one reacting to his adversity in a manner quite opposite from that being urged

45. *Fovre Bookes of Offices: Enabling Privat persons for the speciall seruice of all good Princes and Policies* (London, 1606), p. 188.

—one who, as Frere Lorens says, "will no þing suffre for impacience." For, antiphonally punctuating Pouerte's lengthy exhortation to self-control are the impassioned outbursts of the sufferer:

> Alasse, where is nowe my golde and fe?
> Alasse, I say, where to am I brought?
> Alasse, alasse, alasse! I dye for thought.
> (ll. 1967-69)
> Fy, fy, that euer I sholde be brought in this snare!
> (l. 1972)
> Alasse that euer I sholde be so shamed!
> Alasse that euer I Magnyfycence was named!
> Alasse that euer I was so harde happed
> In Mysery and Wretchydnesse thus to be lapped!
> (ll. 1982-85)
> Alasse! with colde my lymmes shall be marde.
> (l. 2004)
> Fye on this worlde full of Trechery!
> That euer Noblenesse sholde lyue thus wretchydly!
> (ll. 2020-21)
> Alas! of Fortune I may well complayne.
> (l. 2030)

This unrelieved anguish, so typical of the dramatic lament in early English drama and here intensified by the aureate rhetorician's insistent anaphora in expressing it, characterizes Magnyfycence as excessively impatient at this point. Just as the overtones of Herodian bombast in the king's prosperous soliloquies would have evoked for an English audience the familiar image of that boastful tyrant[46] and thus ironically foreshadowed his inevitable fall, so here the char-

---

46. A. R. Heiserman, *Skelton and Satire* (Chicago, [1961]), pp. 84-85, 113.

acteristics of impatience seem designed to foreshadow the inevitable despair that his audience would be expected to associate with such conduct.

Two emphases characterize the lamentations of Magnyfycence during these first outbursts. One is the fact that his suffering is the result of an acute awareness of material loss and physical privation, not of any spiritual inadequacy usually associated with *tristitia* (as in the case of Spenser's knight or Milton's Samson). Also present here at the outset, and modified only by an occasional murmur of self-reproach (l. 1986), is his tendency to indict forces beyond himself for his condition. Beginning with the subtle implications of a passive voice ("Alasse, I say, where to am I brought?" "Fy, fy, that euer I sholde be brought in this snare!" "Alasse that euer I sholde be so shamed!"), this blaming of fate breaks out into the explicit anger of "Fy on this worlde full of Trechery. . . . Alas! of Fortune I may well complayne" and creates an ironic counterbalance to his earlier boasts at the peak of success that

> Fortune to her lawys can not abandune me;
> But I shall of Fortune rule the reyne.
> I fere nothynge Fortunes perplexyte.
>
> (ll. 1459-61)

While Pouerte lectures on at length, these two refrains find expression only in the king's occasional interruptions. But when Pouerte leaves and Magnyfycence is momentarily alone, both ideas combine in a soliloquy that gives them unmistakable prominence. One stanza of rime royal picks up, in an *ubi sunt* formula, the concern for material losses:

> Where is nowe my Welth and my noble estate?
> Where is nowe my treasure, my landes, and my rent?
> Where is nowe all my seruauntys that I had here a late?

Where is nowe my golde vpon them that I spent?
Where is nowe all my ryche abylement?
Where is nowe my kynne, my frendys, and my
   noble blood?
Where is nowe all my Pleasure and my worldly
   good?
(ll. 2055-61)

A companion stanza turns the indictment of Fortune into a strident wail:

O feble Fortune, O doulfull Destyny!
O hatefull Happe, O carefull Cruelte!
O syghynge Sorowe, O thoughtfull Mysere!
   O rydlesse Rewthe, O paynfull Pouerte!
   O dolorous herte, O harde Aduersyte!
      O odyous Dystresse, O dedly Payne and Woo!
      For worldly Shame I wax bothe wanne and bloo.
(ll. 2048-54)

Completely overshadowed, as earlier, in a single brief note of self-accusation ("Alasse my Foly! alasse my wanton Wyll!" [l. 2062]); but it is this as yet dormant awareness of sin that is later to dominate the king's consciousness at the nadir of his despair. Skelton's careful inclusion of this foreshadowing hint, in a deliberately extraneous couplet appended to the two balanced stanzas, is indicative of the meticulous architectonic design of these scenes so often dismissed as mere excess verbiage, beyond the dramatist's real thematic concerns.

Following this soliloquy, which marks the end of the sufferer's doctrinal instruction, occur two parallel scenes in which Magnyfycence is subjected to increased torments. Lyberte returns to mock him, but at the same time constructively to rebuke him for his prosperous follies; then the parasitic courtier-vices reappear to ridicule him, but without any of the moralistic overtones that mark Lyberte's interlude. Consistent with the pattern established during the scenes with Aduersyte and Pouerte and designed to give this section of the play its characteristic effect, Magnyfycence in abject immobility responds very little to those who find him in his misery, the dialogue in both mocking scenes being dominated by those who heap coals upon him. Following each interlude, however, the king bursts forth in a brief soliloquy whose stanzaic form and lamenting tone suggest its balance with, and continuation of, the one that followed the encounter with Aduersyte and Pouerte. It is through these soliloquies especially that one perceives the degenerative course of the hero from impatience to *tristitia* to the threshold of wanhope, as such a course had been defined and analyzed in treatises like the *Somme le Roi* and the parson's sermon in *The Canterbury Tales*.

In the soliloquy that follows the departure of Lyberte, the two dominant ideas of the previous lament are fused and compressed:

> Of worldly Welthe, alasse! who can be sure?
> In Fortunys frendshyppe there is no stedfastnesse;
> She hath dyssayuyd me with her doublenesse.
>
> (ll. 2155-57)

As these diminish, a new note sounds. The king's unreadiness to endure finds its first explicit expression in the anguished cry, "O good Lorde, howe longe shall I indure / This Mysery, this carefull Wrechydnesse?" (ll. 2153-54). Previously he had bemoaned only the present pain and recollection of past felicity; now he recoils at the thought of sustained misery ahead. The outburst not only contrasts with the orthodox view that *"fortitudo* may endure by long suffraunce the travailles that been convenable" but represents in the play the king's overt indication of his falling away from Pouerte's admonition, "All that God sendeth, take it in gre." He has paid little heed to the assurance that "whan it pleaseth God, better may be" (l. 1993).

The next step is, of course, that weariness of life "that sleeth man, as seith St. Paul" in the scriptural passage ("Saeculi tristitia mortem operatur," II Cor. 7:10) cited by Chaucer, St. Thomas Aquinas, and others in discussing Fortitude and its enemy during adversity. Thus, in the next soliloquy, after the vicious mockery of the courtier vices has further intensified his torment, Magnyfycence reaches this dread stage:

Alasse! to lyue longer I haue no delyght;
For to lyue in Mysery, it is herder than Dethe.
I am wery of the worlde, for vnkyndnesse me sleeth.
(ll. 2281-83)

From the beginning of his adversity faced without patience, the wish has lain dormant within him; "Alasse in my cradell that I had not dyde!" (l. 1987) he had complained to Pouerte. But only here does the wish become an articulated expression of *tristitia,* one of the two causes that Chaucer's parson cites as leading to "wanhope, that is despeir of the mercy of God."

No sooner is the readiness for death uttered than Dyspare himself appears allegorically present, proclaiming, "Dyspare is my name, that Aduersyte dothe folowe; / In tyme of Dystresse I am redy at hande" (ll. 2284-85). He proceeds immediately to transform the weariness with life into active self-destruction. His sophistry in doing so, however, is strikingly devoid of references to the ideas that had earlier driven Magnyfycence to *tristitia*. He does not mention the loss of wealth; he says nothing of Fortune's duplicity. As noticed, the king's own outcries have gradually diminished these emphases. The early soliloquy had devoted separate stanzas to each, the middle one had fused them into a single expression representing only part of a stanza, but the third one—that in which the king's world-weariness and readiness for death has just now become explicit—does not refer to either idea. These specific manifestations of the king's impatience in adversity have begotten the more generally pervasive and debilitating condition of weariness with life itself; this weakness of soul Dyspare now exploits by provoking in the king a more acute awareness of his sins, slight indications of which go as far back as the early moments of his despair and have persisted while the wilder accusations of Fortune and former underlings have raged and died out. In the conventional manner, the sense of sin, once exaggerated, leads in turn to disbelief in the redemptive capacity of God's mercy and finally to the desire for death itself. The entire colloquy between tempter and the tempted is relevant:

DYSPARE. What! lyest thou there lyngrynge, lewdly and
        lothsome?
  It is to late nowe thy synnys to repent.
Thou hast bene so waywarde, so wranglyng, and so wroth-
        some,
    And so fer thou arte behynde of thy rent,
    And so vngracyously thy dayes thou hast spent,
      That thou arte not worthy to loke God in the face.
    MAGN. Nay, nay, man, I loke neuer to haue parte
        of his grace;
For I haue so vngracyously my lyfe mysusyd,
Though I aske mercy, I must nedys be refusyed.

DYS. No, no; for thy synnys be so excedynge farre,
   So innumerable, and so full of dyspyte,
And agayne thy Maker thou hast made suche warre,
   That thou canst not haue neuer Mercy in his syght.
MAGN. Alasse my wyckydnesse! that may I wyte!
   But nowe I se well there is no better rede,
   But sygh, and sorowe, and wysshe my selfe dede.
                                        (ll. 2291-306)

The death wish, no longer latent but now active, calls in the figure of Myschefe, who supplies the knife that Magnyfycence is about to use when rescued by divine intervention.

As is true of the stages before it, the temptation of Dyspare conforms in minute detail to the suicidal motif traditionally juxtaposed in opposition to Fortitude. For example, it will be recalled, the gentle parson cites not only "to muche outrageous sorwe" but also "to much drede, ymaginynge that [one] hath doon so muche synne that it wol nat availlen hym" as the causes of "wanhope, that is despeir of the mercy of God." Both of these Skelton has developed into the path of degenerative steps his protagonist follows. In fact, the very sequential order itself is outlined in the *Somme le Roi*, as cited earlier: impatience eventually causes one to fall into *tristitia*, which leads him to desire his own death, so that the devil can induce wanhope and call in Death to slay him (see pp. 111, above).

Of course, this familiar theological concept is by no means limited solely to the context of cardinal virtue discussions on the one hand or to *Magnyfycence* for its literary manifestations on the other. As to the first, its relationship to the virtue of Fortitude is, to be sure, more one of close and longstanding association than of exclusive identity. However, the point to be made is that, while the motif may have appeared outside this context, its repeated association with Fortitude increases the probability that Skelton was working closely within this tradition, the ramification of which would have suggested the pattern for his second conflict just as other associated motifs underlie the action of the first struggle. Present-day assumptions that the latter half of the play has no organic relationship to the earlier scenes may be seen, then, to result from our unfamiliarity with the encompassing tradition of the cardinal virtue that nurtured all these motifs—and numerous others Skelton chose not to develop—within the one subscribing pattern of prosperity and adversity, each with its respective temptation.

Just as there were doctrinal treatises on despair that owed nothing to the cardinal virtues, so there are, besides *Magnyfycence*, numerous literary dramatizations of the idea in varied forms and to various degrees. *The Castell of Labour*, Cordelia's complaint in *The Mirror for Magistrates, Dr. Faustus, The Faerie Queene, Pilgrim's Progress*, and many others have all been cited.[47] Most relevant to an under-

[47] Frederick Ives Carpenter, "Spenser's Cave of Despair: An Essay in Literary Comparison," *MLN*, XVI (1897), 257-73; Harold Golder, "Bunyan's Giant Despair," *JEGP*, XXX (1931), 361-65; and Samuel Chew, *The Virtues Reconciled: An Iconographic Study* (Toronto, 1947), pp. 109-18. Incidentally, Pollet's suggestion that *The Castell of Labour* provides an analogue to *Magnyfycence* (*John Skelton*, pp. 125-26) was anticipated to some extent by Professor Chew's comparative study of the despair motifs developed in these and other pieces. Chew's observations on *The Castell* are relevant to the present study in another way as well. "The Dreamer in this poem," he points out, "does not despair of God's Mercy but is desperate because of his poor condition in the world; he is not burdened with sins, but with poverty and ill success" (*Virtues Reconciled*, p. 116). The suicide of Cordelia in *The Mirror for Magistrates* is, of course, also the result of ill-success in life, whereas most other examples of the motif in the literature of the age stress the sense of sin and loss of faith in salvation. Skelton's unique creativity lies, then, in his

standing of Skelton's play, however, are the other moralities that share this characteristic at the point of the sinner's final struggle. Hardly more than a passing allusion without dramatic development in *Wisdom, Who Is Christ* and in *Nature,* the path of despair is dramatized more fully in *Mundus et infans* and in *Mankynde,* and provides in both, as it does in *Magnyfycence,* the occasion for the second struggle for the soul of the protagonist.

Sister Mary Philippa Coogan's admirable study of *Mankynde* calls attention to the close affinities between this morality and Skelton's at this point.[48] In some ways, *Mundus et infans* is even more analogous. Manhode has attached himself to Foly since the first struggle. Now, after a life in sin has led to his impoverishment, he exclaims in words almost identical to those by Skelton's king under the same conditions:

> Alas, alas, that me is wo!
> My lyfe, my lykynge I haue forlorne;
> My rentes, my rychesse, it is all ygo;
> Alas the daye that I was borne!
>
> (ll. 767-70)

Though the sequence of spiritual degeneration that follows is not developed with the thoroughness that marks Skelton's handling of it, Manhode soon arrives, as Magnyfycence did, at the point of utter despair:

> Alas! Dethe, why lettest thou me lyue so longe?
> I wander as a wyght in wo
> And care.

---

imaginative derivation of the spiritual despair of his hero from the earlier sense of temporal loss into which he had fallen.

48. *An Interpretation of the Moral Play, "Mankind"* (Washington, 1947), p. 60. See also, *Magnyfycence,* ed. Robert Lee Ramsay, EETS, ES, XCVIII (London, 1908 [for 1906]), clxxi.

> For I haue done yll,
> Now wende I wyll
> My-selfe to spyll,
> I care not whyder nor where!
>
> (ll. 804-10)

No diabolical tempters appear to aid in the self-destruction, but Manhode recounts how Folye himself has inculcated in him the sense of excessive shame with which he struggles. Fortunately, Perseueraunce is at hand to prevent the suicide by countering,

> Nay, nay, Manhode, saye not so!
> Be-ware Wanhope, for he is a fo.
> . . . .
> For, and you here repente your synne,
> Ye are possyble heuen to wynne,[49]

just as Good Hope saves Magnyfycence by urging,

> But, my good sonne, lerne from Dyspare to flee;
> Wynde you from Wanhope and aquaynte you with me.
> . . . .
> There was neuer so harde a storme of Mysery
> But thrughe Good Hope there may come remedy.
>
> (ll. 2339-40, 2343-44)

After rescue, all three morality heroes undergo for the remainder of each play a program of re-edification that is also part of the convention, as readers of *The Faerie Queene* will recognize.

Skelton's handling of this regenerative process is significant chiefly because of the attitude *de contemptu mundi*

---

49. Ll. 854-55, 858-59. Citations of *Mundus et infans* are from *Specimens of Pre-Shakespearean Drama*, ed. John Matthews Manly (Boston, 1897), I, 378, 380, and 381.

expressed there, an attitude that has especially puzzled modern critics because of its alleged incompatibility with the play's worldly advice. I shall discuss the point in some detail in the following chapter but, for now, would call attention only to a passage appropriate to the concerns of this chapter. Not only has it been shown that the cardinal virtue with which Magnificence is associated provides the play a unifying principle that necessitates and thus validates both morality conflicts in spite of their superficial disparity, but allusions in the dialogue itself have been shown to bring this larger design into perspective at strategic points by foreshadowing or recalling the play's full course through both crises. Such passages are of no little importance in indicating the dramatist's own architectonic aims. One such instance occurs with great clarity in the speech of Good Hope as he directs the rescued king's attention back over the path he has come. When he urges, "Put fro you Presumpcyon and admyt Humylyte, / And hartely thanke God of your Aduersyte" (ll. 2361-62), he carries us back beyond the problems Magnyfycence has just encountered in the second trial and recalls as well the temptation of prosperity. Continuing, he reveals the mysterious purposes of God which have been present within *both* conditions:

> Prosperyte by Hym is gyuen solacyusly to man;
> Aduersyte to hym therwith nowe and than;
> Helthe of body his besynesse to acheue;
> Dysease and sekenesse his conscyence to dyscryue;
> Afflyccyon and Trouble to proue his Pacyence;
> Contradyccyon to proue his Sapyence;
> Grace of assystence his Measure to declare. . . .
>
> (ll. 2367-72)

As the limited concerns of the second temptations come to be seen in this larger perspective, the play broadens toward the epilogue with its hammerlike insistence upon the full design, just as in reverse the prologue's breadth had narrowed through the opening *débat* to focus upon the limited concerns which then dominated the action of the first conflict. An integrity of design so meticulously emphasized should not be overlooked and can be appreciated only in the light of Skelton's creative reconciliation of morality structure with the ethical theme inherent in the cardinal virtue he felt his king to be neglecting.

5 · Three Interpretive Problems Solved

Just as an understanding of the cardinal virtue of Fortitude (or Magnanimity or Magnificence) explicates both the terminology and, far more significantly, the organic design of the play, so it also provides solutions to many of the lesser enigmas that have baffled modern critics. Furthermore, a resolution of these isolated problems tends to confirm how cohesively all aspects of the play seem to arise out of this one tradition of Stoic-Christian ethics upon which the whole rests. In the present chapter, I shall deal with three of these isolated problems and show the extent to which the basic tradition provides resolutions to them all.

I

One of the cruxes that most troubles the reading of *Magnyfycence* is that posed so clearly by Willard Farnham. Accepting Ramsay's theory that the play is basically an Aristotelian one teaching the preservation of princely wealth by measured dispensation of this world's goods, he finds the theme strangely receiving "the sometimes dubious support" of what he labels as the "Christian-Stoic" convention of mistrusting Fortune's smiles and of adopting an attitude *de contemptu mundi*. "One might think," he suggests, "that Skelton could have small place for the Christian figure of fickle Fortune in this rather well-ordered Aristotelian world. But not so," for the play, especially in its latter stages on adversity, contains "much talk about the wanton turning of Fortune's wheel." The seeming contradiction reaches its ultimate as

> the play actually ends, despite its generous measure of neo-Aristotelian paganism, with an emphatic epilogue *de contemptu mundi* . . .
> Sodenly thus Fortune can both smyle and frowne,
> Sodenly set vp, and sodenly cast downe.
> . . . .
> To day a lorde, to morrowe ly in the duste:
> Thus in this worlde there is no erthly truste.

Skelton is carried away by this conventional condemnation which he has conjured up for things worldly; but, to do him justice, he has made some slight explanatory preparation for its inclusion in a play which bases itself upon Aristotle's balanced worldly wisdom. As he makes Felicity say in the beginning, man can have much control over material prosperity by the use of reason, but man must always remember that wealth is not eternal and that he must not fix his affection upon it too strongly:

> A man may haue Welthe, but not as he wolde,
> Ay to contynewe and styll to endure.[1]

The incompatibility of views is indeed an awkward one for the reader who assumes the play to be one "which bases itself upon Aristotle's balanced worldly wisdom." Since this assumption has been shown to be a less likely one, however, than that which posits for the play an ethical basis in the cardinal virtues which bear the same "Christian-Stoic" label assigned the *contemptus mundi* attitude, might

---

1. Willard Farnham, *The Medieval Heritage of Elizabethan Tragedy* (Berkeley, Calif., 1936), pp. 217-22.

it not be well to restudy the problem in light of this theme? First, however, it is worth noting that the disposition on the part of Skelton to moralize upon the transience of kingly felicity, even to advise Henry himself on the subject, had been one of long standing with him. As early as his elegy, "Of the Death of the Noble Prince, Kynge Edwarde the Forth" (1483), he had that monarch say in a complaint from beyond the grave:

> What is it to trust on mutabilyte,
>   Sith that in this world nothing may indure?
> For now am I gone, that late was in prosperyte:
> To presume thervppon, it is but a vanyte.
>   (ll. 18-21. Dyce, I, 2)

When, later, he came to refurbish a treatise he had prepared for his young student-prince and to present it to the newly crowned Henry VIII as a *Speculum principis,* the poet stressed this same point time and again. If there can be said to be a dominant theme in the *Speculum principis,* which spews its varied maxims like a shotgun, it is embodied in the view expressed early in the piece: "Principes igitur, mea sentencia, attenciori animo immercessibili virtutis gloria quam vana diuiciarum superbia suam vitam componerent."[2] The passage is followed by a host of reiterations advocating the princely rejection of the vain pride of riches in favor of immutable virtue, but by far the most fully developed exemplum of it is one which parallels the action of *Magnyfycence* with extraordinary exactness. It is the story of Saul, who, according to Skelton's interpretation, came to the throne and (like Magnyfycence) "primula sue virtutis florida imago duxit in regum" but who (again like Mag-

2. F. M. Salter, "Skelton's *Speculum Principis,*" *Speculum,* IX (1934), 33. (Fol. 6ʳ.)

nyfycence) "Postea tamen factus elatus, pompa seductus et fastu glorioso." As a result he suffers reverses in fortune ("volente deo," just as Aduersyte and Pouerte in the play are God's agents of correction) and commits the suicide barely avoided by Magnyfycence. This interpretive shaping of the Saul story in such a way that it almost foreshadows the coming morality play is in itself indicative of Skelton's bent in the treating of kings. However, much more to the point at the moment is the moral he draws from the story: "Quamobrem sumopere principibus inuigilandum est virtutem, probitatem, scienciam, doctrinam, et disciplinam sibi acquirant si hic temporaliter cum felicitatis gracia et alibi eternaliter cum immortalitatis gloria regnare decreuerint."[3] That the story he has told bears no clear indications of such a truth to be drawn from it he cares not a whit. This is the conclusion he wishes to draw; this is the kind of advice *de contemptu mundi* he most wants to impress upon his royal charge.

To impress it more tellingly he takes next the direct approach, addressing Henry as "princeps magnificentissimus" and warning him of the almost infinite variety of ways in which his present state of felicity could turn to dust. The warning thunders in an outburst of *reimprosa,* so like the Skeltonics he adopts in English when charged with passionate conviction:

> vulnera funera miserabilia,
> suspecta tempora formidabilia,
> occulta odia inestimabilia,
> factis contraria,
> verba civilia,
> horrida bella execrabilia . . . .

3. *Ibid.,* pp. 34-35. (Fol. 14^r-16^r.)

Still clinging to the same rhyme after a dozen inflections, he climaxes the whole with the doctrine *de contemptu mundi* upon which he was also to close his play:

> fortuna statuit nulla stabilia,
> prospera diu non durabilia,
> aspera aduersa importabilia,
> nunc bona nunc mala semper mobilia—
> cuncta sub sole sunt mutabilia.[4]

As tutor and self-appointed guardian of his king's behavior, Skelton subscribed very emphatically at that time to this doctrine felt by modern readers to be so at odds with the temporal advice purportedly at the heart of *Magnyfycence,* written apparently for Henry's edification only a few years later. However explained, the play's emphasis on the doctrine seems to stem from the poet's lifelong convictions on the point. But is the concept any more intrinsically compatible with the theme of Fortitude than with the Aristotelian interpretation against which it seems such a blemish? The answer is that, from the *De officiis* on, *contemptus mundi* was a major component of the virtue system enabling one to preserve equanimity during prosperity and adversity.

In his very first reference to Fortitude in the *De officiis,* Cicero speaks of it as consisting both of "magnitudo animi" and of "humanarum . . . rerum contemptio."[5] He stresses

---

4. *Ibid.,* p. 35. (Fol. 18ʳ-19ʳ.) The passage is, of course, written in prose; I have taken the liberty of ordering the rhymed periods into an approximation of verse form.

5. i. 4. 13. Centuries later, in the manuals of religious instruction noticed to be one of the means of propagating the cardinal virtue doctrines to the populace, this emphasis upon contempt of the world as part of Fortitude, and especially as associated with magnanimity, continued to be a strong element—even when Macrobian *partes* had become preferable to Cicero's (in spite of the *Summa theologica*) and after Fortitude as

the same duality when later he analyzes the virtue in detail (i. 18. 61). Consequently, it seems more than accidental that, toward the end of his play, Skelton has the virtue of Perseueraunce complete the re-edification of the chastened king by advising him, on the one hand, "fumously adresse you with Magnanymyte" (l. 2493) and, on the other, "Set not all your affyaunce in Fortune full of Gyle; / Remember this lyfe lastyth but a whyle" (l. 2496-97). Quite clearly, the advice is predicated upon the dual components of Cicero's Fortitude. The response of Magnyfycence to it is quite revealing. Having replied to the other, more practical advisors (Redresse and Sad Cyrcumspeccyon) by assuring them that "in my remembraunce your lesson shall rest" and "I marke [you] in my mynde," he concludes more emphatically, "But, Perseueraunce, me semyth your probleme was best; / I shall it neuer forget nor leue it behynde" (ll. 2498-2501). The greater significance expressed for "magnitudo animi . . . humanarumque rerum contemptio" is no accident but a proper subordination of the play's practical concerns to the more inclusive ethic from which the drama has its being.

Before developing the point further, however, I would digress momentarily to comment on Perseueraunce, the character who enters the play here at the end with the sole function of giving the king this moral guidance which he, in turn, swears henceforth to follow. Ramsay was nearer to the truth than he seems aware, not only with respect to the character but about the whole play as well, when he cited as an analogue to Skelton's *dramatis persona* the definition from *The Kalender of Shepherdes* (1506) that "Perseuer-

---

gift had swallowed up Fortitude as cardinal virtue. See, for instance, Dan Michel's *Ayenbite of Inwyt*, ed. Richard Morris, EETS, OS, XXIII (London, 1866), pp. 161, 164-65, 181.

ance is a uertue that establysheth and confermeth the courage by a perfeccyon of vertues that is in a man, and ben perfyte by force of longanymyte."[6] The definition, taken from the context of a discussion of the cardinal virtues in *The Kalender,* actually goes ultimately back to Hugh of St. Victor,[7] who seems first to have supplied explicit definitions for the *partes* of Fortitude as Macrobius had listed them in his Commentary on the *Somnium Scipionis.* But, as Ramsay's other citation suggests, the convention behind the character is somewhat broader than this, though still clearly within the context of the cardinal virtues. For, as he points out, Skelton's Perseueraunce is at the same time the "equivalent to Chaucer's 'constaunce,' one of the five 'speces of fortitude' in the *Parson's Tale* (l. 735), defined as 'stablenesse of corage' " (p. xxxix). That Ramsay was right in perceiving the continuity of the virtue itself, even when the terminology shifts, is indicated by an important passage from the *Summa theologica* in which St. Thomas, wrestling manfully to reconcile the similar but divergent lists of subordinate virtues to Fortitude cited by Cicero and Macrobius, says that Macrobius' *constantia* is actually related to both Cicero's *magnificentia* and his *perseverantia.*[8] In the light

6. *Magnyfycence,* ed. Robert Lee Ramsay, EETS, ES, XCVIII (London, 1908 [for 1906]), p. xxxix. For *The Kalender,* see the edition of H. Oskar Sommer (London, 1892), III, 99.
7. "De fructibus carnis et spiritus," *PL,* CLXXVI, 1003. "Perseverantia est quae virtutum quadam perfectione (longanimitate perficiente) confirmat animum, ne ante consecutum finem desistat ab incoepto."
8. II-II, Q128. Having already discussed two sub-virtues that appear in Macrobius' listing but not in Cicero's, St. Thomas continues, "Tertium autem addit, scilicet constantiam, quae sub magnificentia comprehendi potest," and shortly afterwards adds, "Potest etiam constantia ad perseverantiam pertinere." (St. Thomas also decrees that Macrobius' *firmitas* is the same as Cicero's *perseverantia,* a substitution Hugh of St. Victor had silently made somewhat earlier. Such wholesale cross-equivalents were to reach a point of near-chaos by the time manuals in the *Somme le Roi* tradition had come to identify perseverance as magnificence and

of this synthesis, both Chaucer and *The Kalender* (along with many others) are to be understood as defining the same virtue that Skelton dramatizes; but the significant factor once again is that all the works cited have a common ground in the cardinal virtue of Fortitude.

Consistent with these definitions so understood, Perseueraunce in *Magnyfycence* appears to "establish and confirm" the king's newly attained "corage," and to do it by perfecting him in virtue, not just in matters of financial competence. Since this can be achieved only "by force of longanymyte," the king has properly responded to the indoctrination of Perseueraunce by pledging that "from hym my corage shall neuer flyt" (l. 2465) and repeats, "I shall it neuer forget nor leue it behynde, / But hooly to Perseueraunce my selfe I wyll bynde" (ll. 2501-2). These pledges to adopt an attitude *de contemptu mundi* become reality when, at the closing of the play, the king affirms that "none estate lyuynge of hymselfe can be sure, / For the Welthe of this worlde can not indure" (ll. 2559-60), echoing the fundamental truth introduced in the prologue but forgotten during the action to follow. Paradoxically, upon this late affirmation of other worldliness, his instructors immediately join chorus to certify his preparedness now to rule in *this* world:

> Nowe semyth vs syttynge that ye then resorte
>   Home to your paleys with Ioy and Ryalte.
> Where euery thyng is ordenyd after your noble porte.
>   There to indeuer with all Felycyte.
>
> (ll. 2561-64)

---

even to replace *firmitas* with "hunger and thirst after righteousness," which had infiltrated the previously classical terminology when Fortitude was aligned in the septenaries in conjunction with that particular beatitude. See, for example, Morris, ed., *Ayenbite of Inwyt*, pp. 164, 168-69.)

Just this sudden shifting of emphasis from a detachment from the world to a renewed royal involvement in it is what disturbs modern readers. However, the sequence is precisely the one established as proper by Cicero, who insists that the efficient cause (Caussa ... efficiens) which truly forms a man of Fortitude is "rerum externarum despicientia," or, as Skelton's friend Robert Whittinton translates it, "contempt of outwarde and transytory thynges." Only "whan thou arte so bende in thy mynde" (*cum ita sis affectus animo*) that you do not "couche to fortune" (*fortunae succumbere*), he explains, are you prepared to undertake those worldly responsibilities from which derive "splendor omnis, amplitudo, addo etiam utilitatem" associated with true greatness of soul.[9] Thus, after acknowledging the achievement of those philosophers who attain to this tranquility of mind which enables them to retire from the world's glittering but mutable arena, he goes on to say,

> ... sed et facilior et tutior et minus aliis gravis aut molesta vita est otiosorum; fructuosior autem hominum generi et ad claritatem amplitudinemque aptior eorum, qui se ad rem publicam et ad magnas res gerendas accommodaverunt.
>
> . . . .
>
> Sed iis, qui habent a natura adiumenta rerum gerendarum, abiecta omni cunctatione adipiscendi magistratus et gerenda res publica est; nec enim aliter aut regi civitas aut declarari animi magnitudo potest. Capessentibus autem rem publicam nihil minus quam philosophis, haud scio an magis etiam, et magnificentia et despicientia adhibenda sit rerum humanarum, quam

[9]. *The thre bookes of Tullyes offyces* ... (London, 1534), [D.5ᵛ-D.6ʳ]. For the Latin text, I depend, as always, upon the edition of C. Atzert (Leipzig, 1958).

> saepe dico, et tranquillitas animi atque securitas, si quidem nec anxii futuri sunt et cum gravitate constantiaque victuri (i. 21. 70-72).

The appeal of such a view to writers of Skelton's own age is indicated by La Primaudaye's echo of it in *The French Academie,* when he asserts that,

> whosoeuer hath this vertue of *Fortitude* perfectly . . . he remaineth free from all perturbations of the soule to enioy a blessed tranquillitie, which togither with constancie, procureth vnto him dignitie and reputation. For this cause *Cicero* teacheth vs, that they which giue themselues to the gouernment of affaires, ought (at least asmuch as Philosophers) to make light account of temporall goods, from whence proceedeth all the rest of our mindes; yea, they ought to striue to that end with greater care and labor than Philosophers do, bicause it is easier for a Philosopher so to doe. his life being lesse subiect to *Fortune,* & standing in lesse need of worldly Goods, than doth that of Politicks (p. 270).

Far from being at odds with the play's theme, then, the attitude *de contemptu mundi* so prominent during the period of Magnyfycence's education for renewed kingship is not only consistent with, but fundamental to, the theme—if that theme is rightly understood as dealing with the cardinal virtue of Fortitude rather than with Aristotelian liberality alone. Thus the king, finally "Comprehendynge the worlde casuall and transytory" (l. 2506) and able thereby to rise at last above both pleasure and pain, is the man most capable of returning to his palace as a prosperous ruler.

However, it must not be assumed that this idea is only huddled into the educational process with which the play ends. The care with which the dramatist has woven this strand into the full texture of his play becomes increasingly admirable as one perceives its organic relationship with the whole. For example, one becomes aware that the "much talk about the wanton turning of Fortune's wheel," to which Professor Farnham reacts in the latter stages of the play, actually begins with its obverse, rather suddenly as a matter of fact, when Magnyfycence first adopts his Herodian tone on the pinnacle of felicity:

> Fortune to her lawys can not abandune me;
> But I shall of Fortune rule the reyne.
> I fere nothynge Fortunes perplexyte.
> (ll. 1459-61)

At this point, Fortuna first enters the script to loom ominously behind the ruler who has been led by his flatterers to assume that his prosperity is secure—to forget the play's opening warning that "A man may haue Welth, but not as he wolde, / Ay to contynewe and styll to endure." As La Primaudaye asserts (in paraphrasing a passage in the *De officiis*), the sycophant during prosperity leads one through pleasurable distractions to the threshold of such folly while "on the contrarie side our true friends would lead vs backe to consider *the inconstancie of humane things,* to the ende that we abuse not our felicitie" (see p. 94, above). So Skelton had stressed to Henry the "inconstancie of humane things" by presenting to him the *Speculum principis,* with its reiterated warnings. But within the play, such honest counselors have been silenced and the king has abused his Felicitie and come to "truste to moche to [him] selfe."

The only remedy, according to the Ciceronian pattern, is the hardship of adversity, "to thentent they may se the fragylite of transytory thynges, and dyuers chaunge of fortune."[10] Consistent with this design, as noticed in the previous chapter, Aduersyte comes to render the chastisement, pointing out as he does so "howe Fortune on hym hath frounde"; and Pouerte especially tries to help Magnyfycence "se the fragylite of transytory thynges, and dyuers chaunge of fortune" by lecturing,

> Syr, remembre the tourne of Fortunes whele,
> That wantonly can wynke, and wynche with her hele.
> Nowe she wyll laughe; forthwith she wyll frowne;
> Sodenly set vp and sodenly pluckyd downe;
> She dawnsyth varyaunce with mutabylyte,
> Nowe all in Welth, forthwith in Pouerte.
>
> (ll. 2022-27)

The much talk about the wantonness of Fortune's wheel which occurs during these late scenes represents more than the poet's being carried away illogically by this medieval convention. It arises, instead, quite logically out of the very pattern upon which the play is designed.

Magnyfycence, at this point, has no more matured to an awareness that suffering is temporal than he was able to accept the fact that felicity might pass. Unable to rise above his suffering by a contempt for that which is transitory, he takes no comfort from encouragements that "better may be" and that God is able to "brynge you agayne out of Aduersyte." Futilely blaming Fortune during the soliloquies that follow, he is driven to questioning "how longe shall I indure" that which seems interminable. Suicide is the ultimate refuge. However, salvation from it is followed by that re-educational process in which, as noticed earlier, the most basic advice is to "Set not all your affyaunce in Fortune full of Gyle;/ Remember this lyfe lastyth but a

10. *Ibid.*, F2r.

whyle." Trained at last by his "true friends [who] would lead [him] back to consider the inconstancie of humane things, to the end that [he] abuse not [his] felicitie," Magnyfycence is returned to his palace, exemplifying that prince whom Hoccleve envisions in his treatment of Fortitude (or "magnanimitie," as he calls it)—that prince who, "yf he lordschipës haue, or grete richesse, / Or þat fortunës stynge hym ouerthwerte, / . . . settiþ litel by good temperel" (ll. 3908-9, 3912; p. 141). Understood in this light, *contemptus mundi* is architectonically consistent with both thematic intent and structural design during those portions of the play when its presence is relevant.

2

Another of the troublesome cruxes that must be circumvented in reading the play as a morality dramatizing the Aristotelian mean of liberality is the fact that Aristotle is not the classical authority for "measure" cited within the play. When the character of Measure himself comes upon the scene while the basic issues are being introduced and argued in the opening *débat,* he begins his successful mediation by an analytical discourse upon the golden mean, which he represents. The concept is a central one in the drama and is, of course, a commonplace usually associated with the *Nicomachean Ethics.* Yet Measure begins by citing as his authority among the ancients, not Aristotle at all, but Horace:

> Oracius to recorde in his volumys olde,
>   With euery condycyon Measure must be sought.
>
>   (ll. 114-15)

Professor Ramsay, convinced of an Aristotelian theme, understandably dismisses the allusion as nothing "more than a chance quotation" (p. xxxvii). Yet, for all its strange unexpectedness—indeed, because of this very fact—the reference deserves closer attention.

Actually, the exhortation that "with euery condycyon Measure must be sought" may be found twice in the odes of Horace. According to Ode 10, Book II, "whoever loves the golden mean" (*auream quisquis mediocritatem diligit*) is secure in the midst of life's viscissitudes, for "a well-provided breast hopes in adversity, and fears in prosperity." Thus, advises the poet, you should "in narrow circumstances appear in high spirits, and undaunted. In the same manner you will prudently contract your sails, which are apt to be too much swollen in a prosperous gale." Similarly, Ode 3 of that book begins: "Be mindful to preserve a temper of mind even in times of difficulty, as well as restrained from insolent exultation in prosperity."[11]

Ramsay noted the first of these odes in passing, before dismissing it with the observation that "the *mediocritas* of Horace's worldly wise philosophy has in reality little to do with an ethical principle" (p. xxxvii). However, such a view is at odds with the conclusions reached by a noted critic of the odes, who recently cautioned that "Horace's much publicized Golden Mean is not an invitation to easy compromises, but rather a strategy for weathering life's inevitable extremes." Quoting the very odes in question, he goes on to say that the poet's words "urge a kind of self-regulation, and equable acceptance of fortune or misfortune without surrender to either."[12] Such an ethical principle is far more compatible with Skelton's larger design than is the familiar Aristotelian one concerning the reasonable

11. Translation by Christopher Smart, as revised by T. A. Buckley (New York, 1875), pp. 49 and 42.
12. Steele Commager, *The Odes of Horace: A Critical Study* (New Haven, Conn., 1962), p. 262.

moderated conduct that enables one to be courageous rather than either foolhardy or cowardly, to be generous rather than either prodigal or niggardly, etc.

For that matter, Skelton is quite specific in emphasizing the relevance of the Horatian ideal to his intended action. In making the allusion, the poet stresses that man must have measure "with euery condycyon," a phrasing that suggests and thus underscores Horace's concern for "weathering life's inevitable extremes." These extremes remain in perspective as Measure goes on first to warn that "Welthe without Measure wolde bere hymselfe to bolde" (l. 116) and in this way foreshadows the play's first struggle. Then, before the scene is over, a parallel anticipation of the second struggle occurs in the prophecy that

... without Measure, Pouerte and Nede
Wyll crepe vpon vs, and vs to Myschefe lede;
   For Myschefe wyll mayster vs yf Measure vs forsake.
                                                                        (ll. 152-54)

Faced without measure, times of wealth lead one to boldness and presumption; faced without measure, times of poverty lead one to "Myschefe" (or suicide). Once again, as so often noticed in the previous chapter, the dramatist carefully adumbrates the full range of his dramatic action, this time glossing his cryptic allusion to Horace to suggest its particular appropriateness to the whole.

Most significantly of all, not only does the ideal cited from Horace coincide precisely with the thematic-structural design of *Magnyfycence* but its connection with the cardinal virtue of Fortitude is overwhelmingly attested. This is not to say that Horace intended any such specific association. However, the question at issue is not what Horace intended but what generations of medieval and renaissance moralizers and synthesizers had come to assume concerning the two odes. From the twelfth century on, the poetry of Horace had been ransacked, dismantled, and moralized to provide antique glosses to the cardinal virtues. The *Moralium dogma philosophorum* seems to have established the custom. Structured on the principle of citing under each cardinal virtue a collection of classical excerpts that exemplify it, this florilegium includes both of the relevant passages from Horace within its section on Fortitude.[13] This rather arbitrary association between Horace's words and the cardinal virtue upon which Skelton structured his play soon became a traditional one, destined to become extremely widespread and to persevere even into the seventeenth century. The *Moralium dogma* itself disseminated the association while experiencing an extraordinary popularity, reflected by well over a hundred extant manuscripts, both Latin and vernacular, as well as by five printed editions, four of them within the decade just before the play. More significantly, the influence of the treatise on other important works gained for the idea wider currency still. Brunetto Latini absorbed it into his treatment of the cardinal virtues in *Li Livres dou Tresor*,[14] as did Giraldus Cambrensis in the *De principis instructione liber*.[15] The treatise by Giraldus, it will be recalled, is one of those in which the cardinal virtue is identified by the name of Magnificence ("Magnificentia vero, quae et fortitudo dicitur"). Here, then, one finds

13. *Das Moralium Dogma Philosophorum des Guillaume de Conches: Lateinisch, Altfranzösisch und Mittelniederfrankisch*, ed. John Holmberg ("Arbeten Utgivna Med Understod av Vilhelm Ekmans Universitetsfond," XXXVII [Uppsala, 1929]), pp. 32-33.
14. Edited by Francis J. Carmody ("University of California Publications in Modern Philology," XXII [Los Angeles, 1948]), pp. 263, 269.
15. Edited by George F. Warner (London, 1891), pp. 30-31.

converging in one treatise the same concept dramatized in the play, the same name given its tested protagonist, and the same allusion to Horace as classical authority.

Even more provocative is the treatment found in the *Speculum doctrinale* of Vincent of Beauvais, who also cites Horace's advise as illustrative of this virtue. In both the *Moralium dogma* and *Li Livres dou Tresor,* Horace's odes are cited during discussions of Fortitude but are subordinated therein to two of the Macrobian "partes" of the virtue—*securitas* and *constantia.* The effect is the same since, for example, Latini defines the latter as "une estable fermetés de corage ki se tient en son proposement. Ses offisses est a retenir fermeté en l'une fortune et en l'autre, si ke l'om se s'eschauce trop par prosperité, et ne soit trop troublés en adversité, mais tiegne le mi" (p. 269). However, it is Vincent who provides by far the most direct and striking interrelation of Horace, magnificence, and the prosperity-adversity pattern. Devoting a lengthy sequence of chapters to a thorough explication of the cardinal virtue, the encyclopedist entitles the first such chapter "De fortitudine" and there defines the virtue as that "que nec adversitatis incursu frangitur: nec blandimento prosperitatis eleuatur." Following this are two chapters designed for ready reference, "De magnificentia ... secundum philosophorum" and "De eodem secundum poetarum," the latter containing the citation from Horace's tenth ode.[16] When one recalls Skelton's admiration of "Vincencius *in Speculo,* that wrote noble warkis" (Dyce, I, 377), the tantalizing possibility arises that the dramatist, planning a work to be entitled *Magnyfycence* and desiring an ancient authority to cite, would have turned logically to

16. *Speculum doctrinale* ([Strassburg, *ca.* 1470]), V. lxxi-lxxiii. (Horace's third ode is cited in Chapter lxxxv, also within the context of the Fortitude discussion.)

this handily arranged reference work, sought out the term, found there "the sayings of the poets concerning it," and selected from among them the one so felicitously appropriate from "Oracius in his volumys olde."

As logical as the possibility might be that Skelton actually used the *Speculum doctrinale* for selecting his allusion to Horace, it must, of course, remain mere speculation; for the citation had become a traditional one when the cardinal virtue was under discussion. As a matter of fact, by the sixteenth century, nearly every important florilegium routinely cited the odes in this connection.[17] Furthermore, indicative not just of the survival of this tradition but of the actual preference for Horace's lines above any others as best illustrating Fortitude, there is Barnabe Barnes's citation of them alone in this connection in his treatise modeled on the *De officiis* and designed, like Skelton's play, to instruct the nobility.[18]

Skelton's allusion, so superficially puzzling to the modern reader, is not really so inexplicable at all, then. It is certainly no "chance quotation." Skelton, like Barnes, and in conformity with a custom centuries old, cites in Horace the acknowledged poetic authority for the virtue (sometimes called Magnificence) which enabled one to resist the temptations of prosperity and adversity. Rightly understood, the allusion, like so many other aspects of the play, confirms the architectonic integrity of the whole.

17. See, for example, Domenico Nani Mirabelli, *Polyantheae* (Strassburg, 1517), p. LXXXIX; Joseph Lang, *Florilegii magni* (London, 1559), p. 1071; Octavianus Mirandula, *Illvstrvm poetarvm flores* (Venice, 1565), pp. 276-77; Simon Harward, *Encheiridion Morale* (London, 1596), p. 74. Both Nani Mirabelli's and Mirandula's collections could conceivably have been used by Skelton, having first appeared in 1503 and 1512 respectively.

18. *Fovre Bookes of Offices* (London, 1606), p. 184.

3

Finally, to be enumerated among those characteristics of the play which receive elucidation from the cardinal virtue tradition is the fact of Skelton's thorough-going modification of a psychomachy which had long been directed toward the question of everyman's salvation in a world of sin. The question of Skelton's *originality* in reorienting the purposes conventionally served by the morality genre is not so much the point. The political and social ends served by Sir David Lindsay and the scientific and educational ones served by Heywood and Redford are, after all, roughly contemporary with Skelton's own. Furthermore, the occasional recovery even now of fragmentary early moralities should remind us of how tenuous must remain all efforts to label Skelton or any other writer of the period as the revolutionary figure who altered the morality for all times. Instead, just the fact of Skelton's emphasis on kingly, rather than merely human, conduct is what is important. For this change of intent is reflected in the virtue system one finds in his play. The Prudentian virtues so long associated with the salvation of everyman have been supplanted there by others appropriate to the instruction of royalty. For the cardinal virtues had indeed come, by Skelton's day, to be thought of as the kingly virtues, the proper means of training rulers and of honoring them, as well as the standard for judging their conduct.

It is difficult and, for the purposes of this study, unnecessary to mark with precision just when in the evolution of the cardinal virtues they came to be felt appropriate to rulers especially. In a broad sense, it was thus from the beginning. While the *De officiis* is addressed not to a monarch but to Cicero's son in the spirit of republican Rome, yet its treatment of the four virtues, and most especially the section on Fortitude, abounds in references to the need for these precepts of conduct in those who govern the state. As we shall notice later, by the time of the renaissance the work had come, whether so intended or not, to be a basic document in the education of princes.

Macrobius' commentary on the *Sommium Scipionis* more directly advocates the four virtues for rulers. Devoting one of the more influential of his chapters to a demonstration of that "blessedness which is reserved for the protectors of commonwealths," he gave succeeding ages their version of the Plotinan hierarchy of virtues (the political, the cleansing, the purified, and the exemplary), not emphasizing, however, the Neoplatonic order of ascension but leveling the whole in order to stress the four virtues in their political manifestation. In such a context, he insists that "his uirtutibus uir bonus primum sui atque inde rei publicae rector efficitur."[19]

As influential in its way as either Cicero or Macrobius, the prolific treatise known after the twelfth century as *De quatuor virtutibus cardinalibus* and attributed to Seneca (but actually by Martin of Braga and entitled *Formula vitae honestae*) also related the virtues to the conduct of kings. Addressed to King Miro of Galicia, who had commissioned it for the use of his courtiers, the treatise maintains that the four virtues "are to be exemplified by the prince."[20]

19. Edited by Franz E. Eyssenhardt (2nd ed.; Leipzig, 1893), p. 518.
20. Cited by Lester K. Born in an introduction devoted to ancient and medieval political thought prefixed to his translation of Erasmus, *The Education of a Christian Prince* (New York, 1936), p. 101. The *Formula vitae honestae* has been edited by Claude W. Barlow in the *Opera omnia* of Martin of Braga ("Papers and Monographs of the American Academy in Rome," XII [New Haven, Conn., 1950]), pp. 204-50. Beginning with the year in which *Magnyfycence* itself seems to have been written, the treatise was published in England five times before mid-century, twice

Reflecting this tradition, the art of the middle ages underwent a shift in symbolism during the Carolingian age. The popular depiction of the psychomachian virtues in the iconographic art before that age was sharply modified as, thereafter, the four cardinal virtues came to be considered especially appropriate to the portrayal of royalty.[21] From the wealth of illustrations cited by Katzenellenbogen as indicative of this trend, I shall cite only the ninth-century dedicatory miniature whose center "fills a diamond-shaped frame which encloses a king.... In the remaining corners the artist has drawn circles which serve as frames for the virtues.... Just as the four circles open into the diamond-shaped central frame, so should the king in the interests of his high office let himself be influenced and filled by the cardinal virtues" (p. 32). Continuing undiminished on into renaissance iconography, the association of these virtues with kingship brings meaningful order to Albrecht Dürer's elaborate drawing for the triumphal car of Maximilian, who is shown encircled by the four virtues and their attendant offsprings.[22] So, too, as Josephine Bennett has shown, Queen Elizabeth's

in translation by Skelton's friend, Robert Whittinton (*STC*, 17498-502).

21. Adolf Katzenellenbogen, *Allegories of the Virtues and Vices in Medieval Art from Early Christian Times to the Thirteenth Century* ("Studies of the Warburg Institute," X [London, 1939]), pp. 31-32. See also Raimond van Marle, *Iconographie de l'Art Profane au Moyen-Age et à la Renaissance et la Décoration des Demeures* (Le Harve, 1932), I, 19ff.

22. Valentin Scherer, *Dürer, des Meisters Gemälde Kupferstiche und Holzschnitte*, Band 4 of *Klassiker der Kunst in Gesamtausgaben* (Berlin and Leipzig, 1906), pp. 362-63. Allan H. Gilbert called attention to the numerous virtue-figures in Dürer's print in *Machiavelli's "Prince" and Its Forerunners: "The Prince" as a Typical Book "de Regimine Principum"* (Durham, N.C., 1938), p. 79; but he failed to observe that they are carefully ordered about the cardinal four who circle close about the Emperor. In his treatise, translated by Barclay as *The Myrrour of Good Maners*, Dominicus Mancinus conceives of the four virtues as wheels of a triumphal chariot suitable only for the greatest of kings ([Av]ᵛ).

portraits were often accompanied by the four.[23] Even the crown of the British monarch came to be interpreted as symbolic of the virtues.[24]

Some of the most elaborate iconography of the four virtues developed in connection with the entertainment and receptions accorded royalty in the sixteenth century. For example, in 1501, London received young Katharine of Aragon to celebrate her proposed marriage to Henry's brother, Prince Arthur, by presenting an extraordinary display of pageantry, in which a complex and erudite iconography urged the practice of the cardinal virtues on the young couple, especially on England's heir, whose very name and astrological sign were associated with the virtues. Just two years later Henry's sister, on her way to marry James IV of Scotland, was greeted by pageants in Edinburgh which highlighted the four virtues. During Henry's own reign, John Rastell, Sir Thomas More and William Lyly were instrumental in preparing a gorgeous such royal-entry for the visiting Charles V; and the king himself ordered prepared for Anne Boleyn's coronation a London decoration which also portrayed the cardinal virtues.[25]

23. *The Evolution of The Faerie Queene* (Chicago, [1942]), pp. 224-25. See, in addition to the instances cited by Mrs. Bennett, Erna Auerbach, *Tudor Artists: A Study of Painters in the Royal Service and of Portraiture on Illuminated Documents from the Accession of Henry VIII to the Death of Elizabeth I* (London, 1954), plate 38.

24. John Ferne, *The Blazon of Gentrie* . . . (London, 1586), pp. 142-43; Barnes, *Fovre Bookes of Offices*, [Ai^v].

25. For a thorough explication of the 1501 London pageantry see Sydney Anglo, "The London Pageants for the Reception of Katharine of Aragon: November 1501," *The Journal of the Warburg and Courtauld Institutes*, XXVI (1963), 53-89; and for the other three occasions, see Robert Withington, *English Pageantry: An Historical Outline* (Cambridge, Mass., 1918), I, 168-69, 174-78, 180-84. Withington cites numerous other such pageants throughout the century and across Europe. See also Frances A. Yates, *The French Academies of the Sixteenth Century* (London, 1947), pp. 159, 246, and plates 14a, 24b.

As one would expect, so strong a tradition was by no means limited to the realm of the pictorial arts. At the same time that it was beginning to manifest itself in Carolingian art, it also began to appear literarily. In the *Via regia,* dedicated to Charlemagne himself, Smaragdus of St. Michel maintains that "regia namque virtus est sapientia. . . . Justitiam regibus et prudentiam, fortitudinem et temperantiam donat" (*PL,* CII, 943). Hrabanus Maurus says of the cardinal four, "Hae itaque virtutes cum omnibus sint necessariae, excellentiae tamen regiae maximum decus ornatumque praestant" and "his itaque quatuor virtutibus quasi solidissimis columnis, omnis regiae dignitatis honos decusque attollitur: feliciterque cuncta gubernatur atque exornatur" (*PL,* CX, 1118). These and similar expressions of that age continued into the next century. Bishop Ratherius of Verona, for example, used the cardinal virtues as a standard for his scalding challenge of a king's fitness to rule. "Rex es? Dignitas, rogo, ipsa te dum delectat, instruat. Sunt quaedam regalis ordinis insignia, quibus sine, etsi nomen utcunque, re tamen vera certe non potest consistere dignitas tanta. His ergo utere, his exercere, his exorare. Esto prudens, justus, fortis et temperatus. Hac quasi quadriga evectus regni fines perlustra; hoc denique curru ista utere in via. . . . Hae quatuor ita regales proprie noscuntur esse virtutes, ut cum his quilibet etiam rusticus, rex non incongrue dici; sine gis, nec ipse universam pene monarchiam obtinens mundi" (*PL,* CXXXVI, 220-22).

So considered, the cardinal virtues quite naturally became a basic part of the education recommended for princes when the genre of books devoted to this purpose began to evolve during the middle ages. Both the *Moralium dogma philosophorum* and the *De principis instructione liber,* for instance, seem designed to indoctrinate English kings with these virtues.²⁶ Egidio Colonna's *De regimine principum*, written at the command of Philip III for the instruction of his son, as well as James Yonge's *The Gouernaunce of Prynces*, both include such instruction, though in neither does it form so dominant a portion of the whole.²⁷ On the other hand, as already noticed (p. 82, above), the entire design of Hoccleve's advice to Prince Hal in the *Regement of Prynces* is patterned about the four virtues appropriate to kingship.

As the outpouring of treatises *de regimine principum* quickened in the humanistic ferment of Skelton's own century, this tendency to give the virtues a central place in the ethical instruction of the nobility increased apace. In the process of suggesting that *The Faerie Queene* was itself first conceived on such a plan, Josephine Bennett cites some eight works in Tudor England alone which inculcate these virtues, often as the major ingredient of the regimen.²⁸ Castiglione has Lord Octavian recommend them as part of the training proposed in the climactic book of *Il Cortegiano*.²⁹ They bulk even larger in the plan of Francesco

26. Ph. Delhaye argues convincingly that the first of these represents the teaching program given to England's Henry II as a young prince ("Une adaptation du *De officiis* au XII⁰ siècle: *Le Moralium dogma philosophorum*," *Recherches de Théologie ancienne et médiévale*, XVI [1949], 256-57). The opening section of Giraldus' book, on the other hand, depicts the ideal king in terms of the four virtues before the remaining sections bitterly attack the same Henry II allegedly instructed in the *Moralium dogma*.

27. *Le Livres du Gouvernement des Rois: A XIIIth Century French Version of Egidio Colonna's Treatise, De regimine principum*, ed. Samuel Paul Molenaer (New York, 1899), pp. 31-59. For Yonge's treatise, see *Three Prose Versions of the Secreta Secretorum*, ed. Robert Steele, EETS, ES, LXXIV (London, 1898), pp. 145-91.

28. *Evolution*, p. 220-21.

29. Baldassare Castiglione, *The Book of the Courtier*, trans. Sir Thomas Hoby, ed. Walter Raleigh (London, 1900), pp. 301-10. See also, appended to the treatise, the list of "Chiefe Conditions and Qualities in a Courtier," where is included the requirement "to have the vertues

Patrizi's *De regno et regis institutione* (Paris, 1518), where three of his nine books are devoted to them. Similarly, Sir Thomas Elyot, in *The Boke Named the Gouernour*, devotes a lengthy portion of the first, and practically all of the third, book to their analysis and recommendation as fundamental to the training of those who help rule.[30] For that matter, the basic designs of both La Primaudaye's *The French Academie* and Barnes's *Fovre Bookes of Offices* are structured entirely upon the cardinal virtues. Lodowick Bryskett's imaginary prince in *A Discovrse of Civill Life* is turned over at the age of fourteen to four "royall schoole-masters" whose sole functions are to teach him each of the virtues in turn.[31] The aim in nearly all of these works is essentially like that announced by Jacques Hurault, who professed in his *Politicke, Moral, and Martial Discourses* "to treat of the

---

of the minde, as justice, manlinesse [i.e., fortitude], wisdome, temperance . . ." (p. 369).

30. Recently, students of *The Gouernour* have failed to notice what Leslie C. Warren had earlier shown in this respect—that the chapters on the dance (Chapters 22-25) in Book I inculcate one of the cardinal virtues (Prudence) and that the first twenty-two chapters of Book III treat the other three ("Patrizi's *De regno et regis institutione* and the Plan of Elyot's *The Boke Named the Governour*," *JEGP*, XLIX [1950], 71-77). Stanford E. Lehmberg, in his *Sir Thomas Elyot, Tudor Humanist* (Austin, Tex., 1960), says erroneously that Book III treats all four cardinal virtues (pp. 69 and 85); and Pearl Hogrefe makes a similar statement in "Sir Thomas Elyot's Intention in the Opening Chapter of the *Governour*," *SP*, LX (1963), p. 139. The misconception results from a failure to note, as Warren does (p. 71), that the closing chapters of Book III deal not with the cardinal virtue of Prudence (or Wisdom, as it was often designated) but with the *intellectual virtues* of Sapience, Understanding, and Experience. Mrs. Bennett notes that Elyot treats Prudence in Book I, but interprets the whole of Book III as concerned with the four cardinal virtues, treated "in a more systematic way." The concluding chapters on Sapience, etc., she interprets apparently as the equivalent to Prudence, since her major concern is to stress the synonymity between Prudence and Sapience during the renaissance (*Evolution*, pp. 220-23).

31. (London, 1606), pp. 62-91.

vertues which are termed Cardinall ... and of the branches depending vpon them ... and to see how good princes haue practised them, and how euill princes for want of making account of them, haue found themselues ill apaid."[32]

So trained, the renaissance nobility, certainly in Tudor England, was expected to exemplify these ideals. Dedicating *The Mirror for Magistrates* to the English nobility, John Higgins stresses these four virtues "whiche are requisite in him that should be in authoritie."[33] A nobleman's place in the elaborate code of heraldry was said to depend upon his exemplification of them.[34] Certainly, Queen Elizabeth gave at least lip service to the concept by saying, on one occasion, that for rulers "nothing is more necessary, then to be plentifully furnished with the predominant Vertues of *Iustice, Temperance, Wisedome,* and *Fortitude*" and, on another, that a king "scant was wel furnished, if either he lacked Justice, Temperance, Magnanimitie, or Judgement."[35]

This literature of princely instruction in the virtues, as one would expect, was largely a derivative amalgam of Cicero, Macrobius, Martin of Braga, the church fathers, and any others deemed worthy to quote or to plagiarize. But far above the rest (unless it be Macrobius) was honored Cicero, especially for his *De officiis,* considered the *locus classicus* for such instruction. As early as the *Moralium dogma philosophorum,* treatises *de regimine principum*

32. Translated by Arthur Golding (London, 1595), pp. 3-4. Even as early as the medieval *Book of Vices and Virtues,* one finds the observation that "bi þes foure vertues ... is a man worþy to be a gouernour, first of himself and siþen of oþere" (ed. W. Nelson Francis, EETS, OS, CCXVII [London, 1942], p. 124).

33. John Higgins and Thomas Blenerhasset, *Parts Added to the Mirror for Magistrates,* ed. Lily B. Campbell (Cambridge, 1946), p. 32.

34. John Bossewell, *Workes of Armorie* (London, 1572), 4ʳ; Gerard Legh, *The Accedens of Armory* (London, 1568), "The Desscripcion of the Viniet"; Ferne, *Blazon of Gentrie,* p. 30.

35. Bennett, *Evolution,* p. 225.

were organized in close imitation of its plan.³⁶ By Skelton's age especially, the respect accorded it in this field can be estimated from the wholesale borrowings made by both Patrizi and Elyot, by the very title of Barnes's work, and by La Primaudaye's imitative structure and almost ceaseless paraphrasing from it. Above all, its pre-eminence accounts for the recommendations by Elyot and others that young noblemen should learn their moral philosophy directly from the *De officiis*.³⁷

Such recommendations were not rhetorical merely; Elyot's advice was practiced in the royal family of Tudors. Henry VIII's own son, Edward, underwent a particularly rigorous study of the *De officiis,* especially the opening book with its analysis of the cardinal virtues, from which he was expected to extract *sententiae* for his moral edification.³⁸ That Henry, too, had so labored over the work is strikingly evident from a perusal of his textbook copy of it, which survives today, complete with its interlinear glosses and marginal notes in two hands, one that of the royal student, the other alleged to be that of his tutor—John Skelton (see above, p. 77).

Incidentally, dating from approximately the same time when Skelton seems possibly to have trained the young prince in this Ciceronian model for all treatises *de regimine principum,* he was composing his own work in the same genre—the *Speculum principis* already noted to have striking affinities with certain aspects of his morality play. It

36. Delhaye, "Une adaptation," *Recherches,* pp. 227-58. See also N. E. Nelson, "Cicero's *De Officiis* in Christian Thought: 300-1300," *Essays and Studies in English and Comparative Literature* ("University of Michigan Publications, Language and Literature," X [Ann Arbor, 1933]).

37. Sir Thomas Elyot, *The Boke Named the Gouernour,* ed. H. H. Croft (London, 1883), I, 92-93 (Book I, Chapter 11).

38. T. W. Baldwin, *William Shakespere's Small Latine & Lesse Greeke* (Urbana, Ill., 1944), I, 227-29.

was Professor Ramsay's speculation that, when found, the *Speculum* would turn out to be "in all likelihood the true intermediary between Aristotle and *Magnificence*" (p. lxxviii). It did not prove to be Aristotelian at all. On the other hand, in addition to the *contemptus mundi* strain and the analogue of the Saul story already noticed, it did contain an admonition by now familiar—*"Esto fortis in aduersis, cautus in prosperis."*[39] Taken almost verbatim from Martin of Braga's *De quatuor virtutibus cardinalibus* ("esto ... in adversis firmus, in prosperis cautus"),[40] the aphorism once again provides a clear anticipation of the thematic design of *Magnyfycence*.

When, soon after he had refurbished and presented the treatise to the newly crowned Henry, Skelton began to perceive his "princeps magnificentissimus" obviously disinclined to be "cautus in prosperis," what more appropriate means could he have found for a scholar's reprimand than the classical system of cardinal virtues which, as noticed, had come almost universally to be considered appropriate to the teaching of kings, the ethical system that Henry had studied as a youth, possibly even from the poet himself? The need was for instruction not in all four virtues but in that one proclaimed in instructional literature as being "more generallie followed of princes, than any of the other," the one with which "kings and mighty men ought to be armed,"

39. Salter, "Skelton's *Speculum*," *Speculum*, p. 36. (Fol. 21ᵛ.)
40. IV. 65. Barlow, ed., *Opera omnia*, p. 245. F. M. Salter and H. L. R. Edwards suggest that Skelton drew the aphorism from *Cato's distichs*, where appears
   Tranquillis rebus semper diuersa timeto,
   Rursus in aduersis melius sperare memento
(See their edition of Skelton's translation of Diodorus Siculus' *Bibliotheca Historica*, EETS, CCXXXIX [London, 1957], II, 423-24). However, the wording of the *Speculum principis* is not very close to this couplet, while it is almost identical to that in the *De quattuor virtutibus cardinalibus*.

the one that "instruct[s] the Soueraigne ... so that he be not quailing in his mind, neither by aduerse fortune, nor elated with the prosperous."[41] The felicitous compatibility between this timely subject matter fit for kings and the two-conflict morality structure traditionally used as the vehicle for moral and religious instruction provided the poet with that kind of creative situation he always exploited most successfully, the conventional literary vehicle capable of bold adaptation to new purposes. The result is a morality play designed for the "salvation" of a king, built around the virtue system appropriate to royalty rather than to mankind in general.

Whether it be an apparently extraneous refrain *de contemptu mundi,* an unexplained allusion to Horace, or a new morality-play emphasis upon those virtues traditionally associated with the instructing of princes, each facet of Skelton's drama receives elucidation from the cardinal virtue system from which the whole derives. Thus, problems of such diversity for the modern reader coalesce in a single pattern of explication, and the economy of probability points ever more convincingly to this ethical system as the background appropriate to the play. It cannot, of course, be claimed that the cardinal virtues uniquely explain every aspect of the morality. To cite the obvious, for example, the emphasis on Fortune and a contempt for worldly felicity has, of course, far wider currency than any exclusive association with the concept of Fortitude. So, too, have warnings against flatterers during prosperity or against the

41. Hurault, *Politicke,* trans. A. Golding, p. 275; Jean Cartigny, *The Voyage of the Wandering Knight,* trans. William Goodyear, ed. Dorothy Atkinson Evans (Seattle, 1951), p. 105; Ferne, *Blazon of Gentrie,* pp. 142-43. Similar emphases upon Fortitude for the nobility appear in Bryskett, *Discovrse of Civill Life,* p. 87, and in *The Institvcion of a Gentleman* (London, 1568), Ci^v-Cii^r.

dangers of despair in adversity. However, the traditional handling of each of these within the cardinal virtue context supplies, in each case, the most satisfying understanding of their roles within the play and resolves cruxes otherwise unexplained. As repeated explications converge upon a single strong tradition, the probability increases immeasurably that this, rather than a number of diverse and incompatible sources, represents the ethical dogma chosen for dramatization.

6 · A Concluding Analogue

If, as this study suggests, Skelton modified the conventional morality-play system of virtues to dramatize a virtue fitted for kings, he was not alone in his innovation. For there exists, in fragment, one other morality based not on the psychomachian but on the cardinal virtues; and it too concerns itself with kingly conduct, has a protagonist akin to Skelton's, is built upon a prosperity-adversity design, and even directs its conclusions towards Henry VIII himself. The play, only recently recovered and edited, bears the explicit title, *The Enterlude of the .iiii. Cardynal Vertues, and the Vyces Contrary to Them*, and dates from before 1547, though it may possibly have been written in one form as early as 1528.[1] The multitude of similarities between this work and Skelton's play indicate even further that *Magnyfycence* must be understood in the tradition of the cardinal virtues.

In the first place, while all four of the cardinal virtues appear in the fragmentary morality, it is Fortytude who is the erring central figure just as in Skelton's play the protagonist is Magnyfycence, the important subsidiary virtue to Fortitude and even its sometime equivalent. Furthermore, just as Magnyfycence is not an everyman figure but the embodiment of kingship itself, so Fortytude in the other

[1] Edited by W. W. Greg in *The Malone Society Collections*, IV (1956), 41-54.

play recalls that before his fall "somtyme I was full royall" (l. 128); and, when the other three virtues rescue and reinstate him, they proclaim, "Than with a newe name we wyll the restore / Fortytude thus we the call / ... / In token whereof take this crowne ryall" (ll. 174-75, 178).

In both moralities, the motif of alternating prosperity and adversity is repeatedly stressed. The encompassing structural design built upon this motif which unifies all of *Magnyfycence* has been sufficiently analyzed in earlier chapters. As for *The Enterlude of the .iiii. Cardynal Vertues,* although the fact that only the last two hundred and forty-five lines survive prevents first-hand knowledge of its full design, much can be reconstructed from the dialogue remaining. For example, Fortytude himself recalls that upon his "fyrste commynge in to this hall,"

> ... than aduersytye men dyd me call
> Chaunged into prosperyte by crafte colorable
> Disobedience I was I feared no fall.
> (ll. 186-89)

The lines mean either that he was first in adversity and was deluded "by crafte" into an apparent prosperity from which he (like Magnyfycence) "feared no fall" or that a prosperity he boasted of from the outset was only a veneer of appearance covering the reality of his miserable human finitude, which he would not recognize. The former seems the simpler reading and would suggest a morality opening something like (though not in all things comparable to) that of *Mundus et infans,* in which infelicity precedes felicity, which is then lost and later recovered. In any case, the significant point of comparison to *Magnyfycence* lies in the pattern of alternating conditions that underlies both plays—the pattern conventionally associated with Fortitude.

Whatever the nature of the play's opening, other words by Fortytude in the fragmentary conclusion clearly delineate the sweep downward from prosperity. He recalls that when "somtyne I was full royall / Than prosperytye was my name" (ll. 128-29) but that "nowe I am cast in to this degre / And all is longe of aduersytye" (ll. 163-64). The actor's costume at this point emphasizes the condition, for a speech-heading reads "Fortitu-poorely" (l. 118). Conversely, when the king has been restored and renamed Fortytude, he is given by the virtues not only "this crowne ryall" but "this robe and garment gay" (l. 179), just as Skelton has one of the redemptive figures say to Magnyfycence, "Nowe shall ye be renewyd with Solace; / Take nowe vpon you this abylyment" (ll. 2404-5), and a stage direction indicates that the king *"accipiat indumentum."* With such similitude are both plays constructed so as to adapt the two-phase morality structure to the prosperity-adversity pattern inherent in the cardinal virtue of Fortitude.

Furthermore, if one can feel some implicit address to the spectator, Henry VIII, in Skelton's last minute return of the hero to his palace "There to indeuer with all Felycyte" as well as in the closing benediction, "And ye that haue harde this dysporte and game, / Jhesus preserue you frome endlesse wo and shame" (ll. 2566-67), one is not allowed to miss the extension of the prosperity-adversity motif to include England's lavish king in *The Enterlude of the .iiii. Cardynal Vertues.* For the dramatist has his characters say in benediction:

> Preserue this realme from aduersytye
> And kepe it alwaye in prosperytye
> . . . .
> Ye and lorde Iesu we pray to the
> Dayly to preserue and defende

> Our noble kynge Henry the eyght
> All welth and prosperitie Iesu hym sende.
>
> (ll. 205-6, 211-14)

Supplementing these characteristics shared in common, there are, in addition, the comparable rôles of Lyberte and Wylfull in the two plays. However, before a comparison, must come a contrast. Skelton's Lyberte (whose synonym throughout the play is Wyll) is a character distinct from Magnyfycence, though, allegorically understood, he represents the king's inclination toward a free assertion of his will. However, in *The Enterlude of the .iiii. Cardynal Vertues,* Wylfull is in a sense synonymous with Fortytude, as an analysis of rôle distribution and dialogue will reveal.

From the evidence of the fragment, the play was designed for performance by a troupe of only four actors, barely enough for the cardinal virtues themselves. Thus, the surviving action opens with Wylfull in the captivity of three of the cardinal virtues—all except Fortytude. When Prudence says at one point, "Fortytude I wolde were here" (l. 67), Wylfull announces that "He is my lorde" (l. 70) and volunteers to bring him, if released. When he is freed to do so, there is the stage direction, "Et exeat ad lud' poorely" (l. 96); and soon the same actor returns dressed as "Fortitude poorely," according to the speech-heading already noticed. For the remainder of the play, only the four cardinal virtues appear on stage.

Inherent in this routine change of rôles so typical of morality stagings is a very real thematic intent. For Wylfull actually *is* Fortytude in his vicious manifestations. As noted earlier, when Fortytude appears, he recalls that "somtyme I was full royall"; but before his entrance it is Wylfull who is—or has been—king. It was he who was said to "haue reygned" (l. 37); "He was gyuen great auctorytye . . . and set in degre" (ll. 38-39); "Rex regum he wylled to be" (l. 55). However, "nowe deposed is he" (l. 103). Thus, at the height of his rule Fortytude had become the embodiment of wilfullness. In fact, it may be that only a mutilated page of the surviving text prevents our hearing Fortytude explicitly say that his name has been Wylfull. For his first speech in the fragment is damaged. One line ends with the word "wylfulness"; and, after two lines almost obliterated, the damage decreases so that one can read (and hypothesize) the phrase, "Ne rem[ember I fro] whens I came / Ne knowelege of whome I had that name."[2] It seems quite likely that "that name" he had was "Wylfullness."

Incidentally, if the reconstruction suggested is a valid one, it gives us a sequence of names that the protagonist has borne to mark the stages of his metamorphosis throughout the earlier portion of the play. For it is just after the passage reconstructed that Fortytude says that when he was king "prosperytye was my name," and hard upon that Temperance recognizes him as one he knew as Disobedience, an identity the hero himself admits by saying somewhat later, "Disobedience I was" (l. 189). As noticed earlier, he has also said that when he first appeared on stage, "aduersytye men dyd me call" before he was changed into

2. Ll. 120, 123-24. The bracketed portions represent my own hypothetical reconstruction of a lacuna in the text. The presumption is taken upon the basis of probable meaning and meter as well as upon evidence afforded by slightly earlier lines, which say that "Whan a man is vp brought and set in his aboue / He wyl nat *remembre fro whence that he came*" (ll. 27-28).

It should be noted, also, that some doubtful but visible letters that Greg records in pointed brackets have not been so indicated in my quotations. In other quotations I have also silently corrected inverted letters that Greg leaves as in the original.

Prosperytye. In addition to these explicit references to earlier names, there is the observation by one of the virtues that "Wylfulnes causeth dysobedience" (l. 108), which provides a final link in the sequence. Reassembled, the sequence seems to have been as follows: the personage who begins the play as Aduersytye is "by crafte colorable" given the name Prosperytye; and then, in some way beyond his later recollection, he receives the name Wylfull, and from this, in turn, he comes to be called Disobedience. How it is that Wylfull, and not Disobedience, is on stage as the fragment begins is not clear. Be that as it may, the sequence reaches its culmination with the announcement by the three virtues to the penitent one that they will give him the "newe name" of Fortytude. Though a person of this name has been longed for by Prudence and gone after by Wylfull (who, of course, never returns), and though speech-headings have borne this name, the last minute christening seems to be the first moment in the play in which the character has been so identified for the audience. He has only now matured his way through prosperity and adversity until for the first time he truly represents Fortytude.

To return to the original comparison, although Wylfull is to be identified with Fortytude in one play while Lyberte is by no means synonymous with Magnyfycence in the other, the psychological allegory conveyed by the terms is quite similar in each case. In the prologue to *Magnyfycence,* for instance, the events immediately ahead are foreshadowed by the warning:

> ... Wyll hath Reason so vnder subieccyon,
> And so dysordereth this worlde ouer all,
> That Welthe and Felicite is passynge small.
>
> (ll. 19-21)

Just so, the retrospective view in *The Enterlude of the .iiii. Cardynal Vertues* is that

> This worlde is combred and brought in wo
> Wylfulnes hath approched this worlde to spyll
> If he myght haue reygned his wyll for to do
> (ll. 35-37)

> Wylfulnes dyd neuer good in dede
> Aduersytye it bryngeth apase
> And causeth welth to stande in drede
> And to be banysshed fro all solace.
> (ll. 104-7)

Temperance and Prudence say of Fortytude in the latter play that

> He wylled to haue bene lorde of all
> So wylfull he was in degre:
> He refused you and also me
> He banysshed welth with loue also.
> (ll. 133-36)

The rejection of these two and the resulting loss of wealth seem to have been specific events in the drama, for Fortytude himself recalls that

> So outragious I began in wilful to be vnstable
> Vnto prudence and temperaunce I was vnkynde
> Also agaynst reason I wrought importunable
> . . . .
> Than was I depryued and brought full lowe.
> (ll. 194-96, 199)

Similarly, Sad Cyrcumspeccyon and Measure are abandoned and rejected by Magnyfycence when he follows the whim of his Lyberte. When, near the play's close, Cyrcumspeccyon reproves the fallen king with, "Cyrcumspeccyon inhateth all rennynge astray. / But, Syr, by me to rule fyrst ye began," the shamefaced answer is, "My Wylfulnesse, Syr, excuse ne I can" (ll. 2430-32). The instance alluded to is, of course, the forged letter from Cyrcumspeccyon. This trick, recalls the king, "caused me also to vse to moche Lyberte, / And made also Mesure to be put fro me" (ll. 2445-46), an allusion to the summary expulsion of Measure from his post as the moderating restraint upon Lyberte.

Unchecked at the time by either of these virtuous influences and confidently assured that "I haue Welth at Wyll" (l. 1458), Magnyfycence had begun immediately to boast of his infallible superiority over any other rulers, even over Fortune herself, and listened to the advice of his flatterers:

> By waywarde Wylfulnes let eche thynge be conuayed;
> What so euer ye do, folowe your owne Wyll;
> Be it Reason or none, it shall not gretely skyll;
> Be it ryght or wronge, by the aduyse of me,
> Take your Pleasure and vse free Lyberte.
>
> (ll. 1594-98)

As already noticed, the fall from Fortune's wheel was immediate. The same postures and the same consequences result from the ascendancy of Wylful in *The Enterlude of the .iiii. Cardynal Vertues*. Prudence, in a monologue of self-analysis, says in effect that while he preserves man from sin,

> Wylfulnes hym tyceth & maketh hym full prone
> He wyll nat remembre what he hase mysdone
> Whan a man is vp brought and set in his aboue
> He wyl nat remembre fro whence that he came
> Who hath hym forth broughte he taketh no leue

But foloweth his own wyl to brynge him to shame
Hye for to clymbe they take it for a game
To regarde theyr power fewe hath a zele
But beware the worlde it turneth as a whele.
                                              (ll. 25-33)

In his contrition, Fortytude accepts this general truth as specifically applicable to his own past career:

Nowe men may se what auayleth wylfulnes
It presenteth man euer to be vnkynde
By me it may be verefyed and ye haue in mynde
. . . .
My myght and my myschefe was intollerable
My purpose exalted to clymbe aboue all
But fortune sone chaunged and turned as a ball
And depryued me fro honour with my wylful minde.
                                       (ll. 183-85, 190-93)

In these and the other instances cited, the allegorical roles of Wylfull and Lyberte are closely comparable, especially in those ways in which they are related to the basic design of prosperity and adversity.

Two further similarities of note between the two plays might be cited. One, more tantalizing than satisfying in its fragmentary suggestiveness, pertains to patience as Fortytude's remedy for suicide. Moralizing as the play closes, Fortytude says in summary that arraigned against the vices are "vertuous opposytes" that enable man not only to turn "fro suche frowarde lyuynge" as his life-in-prosperity has manifested but also "in his herte with perfyte pacyence / [to] take suche assautes done by aduersytye" (ll. 236, 238-39). What these assaults of adversity were in the play (if, indeed, they were literally dramatized), one cannot now be sure; but the second line of the fragment has the imprisoned and humiliated Wylfull (or Fortytude) exclaim in apparent despair, "Nay rather with deth amendes wyll I make." As noticed with respect to *Magnyfycence* and the medieval tradition of the cardinal virtues, it is "perfyte pacyence," the sub-virtue of Fortitude, that most protects man from this "assaute done by aduersytye." Beyond the hint of these two brief passages, however, there is nothing else in the fragment remaining to confirm the dramatized presence of any motif of despair-in-adversity in the earlier scenes now lost.

The other similarity takes us back to the "problem" of the attitude *de contemptu mundi* that closes a play like *Magnyfycence* simultaneously with its hero's return to the earthly felicities of his throne. *The Enterlude of the .iiii. Cardynal Vertues* entails the same apparent contradiction, which is satisfyingly resolved into paradox in the light of the Fortitude tradition, as noted in the preceding chapter. For, by the time Fortytude comes upon the scene in the fragment, he has discovered, as Magnyfycence did, a "[w]orlde with dowblenes / Somtyme [of low or (?)] of hye degre."[3] He has learned that "fortune sone chaunged and turned as a ball"; indeed, it is upon this hard lesson and the devout contrition it produces that he is deemed worthy to receive his "newe name," his "crowne ryall," and his garments symbolic of renewed prosperity, the very condition he has come to recognize as mutable. Next, as noticed, the renewal of worldly felicity is extended, by benediction, to England and especially to "Our noble kynge

3. Ll. 118-19. Again brackets indicate a reconstructed reading based on the four-beat rhythm and on such analogies as "nowe hy, nowe lawe degre; / . . . / So in this worlde there is no Sykernesse" (*Magnyfycence*, ll. 2512, 2517) and "Sodenly set vp and sodenly pluckyd downe; / . . . / All her Delyte is set in Doublenesse" (*Magnyfycence*, ll. 2025, 2029).

Henry the eyght / All welth and prosperitie Iesu hym
sende" (ll. 213-14). The whole is concluded, soon thereafter, with an interpretation of the play which runs diametrically counter to such emphases on this world's goods:

> For surely here ye may se by experyence
> That sone ouertourned this worldly prosperytye
> Therfore I counsell [e]uery degre
> Trust to that welth promysed from aboue.
> (ll. 240-43)

Contradictory it may be to the twentieth-century reader, but the fact is that, deep within the tradition of Fortitude as a cardinal virtue, there was the righting paradox that such a contempt for worldly things could provide the man of Magnanimity with that stability which best fits him for controlling the affairs of state in a world of alternating prosperity and adversity. This fact alone explicates both plays at the crucial point.

Such parallels as have been drawn between the two plays concerning the centrality of a Fortitude figure, the emphasis upon kingship, the prosperity-adversity pattern, the rôle of Will, the possible suicide motif, and the ending *de contemptu mundi* are not intended to imply that the moralities are near-duplicates of each other. There are, to be sure, numerous divergencies of emphasis: no hint of courtier-vices in one play, no reiteration of the doctrine of grace in the other, etc. However, the similarities do tend to suggest that the two morality-playwrights are working in the same general tradition, though their ultimate artistic and moral purposes may differ.

For an appreciation of *Magnyfycence* especially, this kinship in essence is significant in that it tends to confirm what the earlier chapters of this study have shown—that the cardinal virtue of Fortitude, as understood after a long evolutionary development into Skelton's age, answers far better than does the usual Aristotelian interpretation the varied questions raised by this only surviving morality play by the poet. For the anonymous fragment, by the explicitness of its very title, rests unequivocally upon the cardinal virtue tradition; and it happens also to coincide in many important details with the salient features of Skelton's play, the ambiguity of whose title has obscured our modern understanding since it was apparently designed to conceal under a flattering term of royal address a subtle but severe reminder to a prosperously intemperate king that he was not exemplifying the kingly virtue associated with that title.

Understood in this way, rather than as a truncated dramatization of a doubly misunderstood Aristotelian concept marred by a strangely irrelevant conclusion, an epilogue to be ignored, an inexplicable Horatian allusion to be doubted, much contradictory advice on the mutability of worldly felicity, etc., the play can be especially appreciated for its structural integrity, as its two-part morality design is made to serve a theme felicitously compatible with it throughout.

Index

A

Accedens of Armory, The, 69, 152
Accidia (or acedia), 105-14 passim.
  See also Despair, Tristitia
Alanus de Insulis, 79n, 110-11
Albert the Great, 61, 78, 105-6
Alexander of Hales, 80
Ambrose, Saint, 75, 101-2
Andronicus of Rhodes, 65n
Aquinas. See Thomas Aquinas, Saint
Aristotle, his concept of liberality, 6; uncited in Magnyfycence, 10, 87, 139; alleged source for Magnyfycence, 46-50 passim, 57, 58-59, 62-63; Ethics influence cardinal virtues, 60-61, 65-66, 67; and Speculum principis, 153-54; mentioned, 11, 64, 68, 70, 72, 95, 127-28, 131, 136, 140-41, 167-68
Arthur, Prince, son of Henry VII, 77n, 148
Auden, W. H., vi, vii
Augustine, Saint, on suicide and magnanimity, 102-3; influence of, 103, 106, 113; mentioned, 80, 107
Augustine, pseudo-, 80
Avarice, 73
Ayenbite of Inwyt. See Michel, Dan

B

Bale, John, vii, 20
Bang, Willy, vii-viii, 17
Barclay, Alexander, Ship of Fools, 23, 28-29, 37; Myrrour of Good Maners, 68, 69; Castell of Labour, 122; mentioned, 147n
Barlowe, Jerome, 17, 32-33n
Barnes, Barnabe, Fovre Bookes of Offices, on Fortitude vs. despair, 113-14; based on Cicero, 144, 153; cites Horace under Fortitude, 144; relates cardinal virtues to kingship, 148, 151
Bennett, Josephine W., 147-48, 150, 151n
Bevington, David M., ix
Bibliotheca Historica, 30-31
Blazon of Gentrie, The. See Ferne, John
Boke Named the Gouernour, The. See Elyot, Sir Thomas
Boleyn, Ann, 148
Bonaventure, Saint, 78, 110-11
Book of Vices and Virtues, 152n. See also Lorens, Frere
Born, Lester K., 82n, 146
Bossewell, John, 152
Brant, Sebastian. See Barclay, Alexander
Brie, Fredrich, 20
Brutus, 113
Bryskett, Lodowick, equates magnificence-magnanimity-liberality, 68; on prosperity-adversity motif of Fortitude, 84-85; on cardinal virtues for rulers, 151, 155n
Buckingham, Edward Stafford, Duke of, 16, 21

INDEX

Bunyan, John, *The Pilgrim's Progress*, 112, 122

C

Calais, 33, 36-37
Cardinal virtues, in *Faerie Queene*, 64, 67, 150; relation to gifts of the Holy Spirit, 109-10; associated with rulers, 144-55; recently discovered morality play on, 157-67; mentioned, x, 59-70 *passim*. *See also* Fortitude
Cartigny, Jean, 112, 154-55
Cassiodorus, Flavius Magnus Aurelius, 79
Castell of Labour, The, 122
Castiglione, Baldassare, 150-51
Castle of Perseverance, The, 5, 71, 72
Cato, Dionysius, 113, 154n
Charles V, Emperor, 148
Charlemagne, 149
Chaucer, Geoffrey, *The Canterbury Tales*, satire of dress in, 23; on Fortitude vs. despair, 107-9, 118, 119, 121; on perseverance and Fortitude, 113, 134
Christ, 102
Chew, Samuel C., 122n
Cicero, Marcus Tullius, *De inventione*, basis of Thomistic ethic, 59-61; influence of, 59-69 *passim*, 106, 109, 113; defines "magnificence," 60; cites *partes* of Fortitude, 65-66, 69, 131n, 133
—*De officiis*, treats "magnificence," 61; on prosperity-adversity motif of Fortitude, 73-74, 77, 95-96; influence of, 74-78 *passim*, 84-85, 101-4 *passim*, 144, 152-53; Whittinton translation of, 76-77, 84, 88, 96, 135; taught by Skelton to Henry VIII, 77, 153; on flatterers and advisers, 88-89; on Fortitude in adversity, 101; *contemptus mundi* in, 131-32, 135-36, 137-38; as treatise for rulers, 145-46; mentioned, 81, 93, 94, 97, 98

Collier, John Payne, 4, 8
Colonna, Egidio, *De regimine principum*, 150
Commager, Steele, 140
"Complaynte of Northe . . . , The," 16
Contemptus mundi, in *Magnyfycence*, 10, 83, 124-25, 127-29, 131, 132, 134, 136-39, 155, 166; in other Skelton works, 129-31, 154; in *Ayenbite of Inwyt*, 131-32n; in *De officiis*, 131-32, 135-36, 137-38; and Fortitude, 131-32, 135-38, 166-67; in *.iiii. Cardynal Vertues*, 166-67
Coogan, Sister Mary Philippa, 123
Cordelia, 122
Cortegiano, Il, 150-51

D

De civitate Dei, 102-3
Delhaye, Phillippe, 150n
De officiis ministrorum, 75, 101-2
De Patientia, 107
De principis instructione. *See* Giraldus Cambrensis
De quatuor virtutibus cardinalibus. *See* Martin of Braga
De regimine principum, of Egidio Colonna, 150
De regno et regis institutione. *See* Patrizi, Francesco
Despair, in morality plays, 9, 47, 122-24, 165-66; Ramsay inconsistent on, 47; resisted by Fortitude, 101-14, 121-22; road to, dramatized in *Magnyfycence*, 108, 111-12, 114-21, 124
De spiritu et animi, 80
De vita contemplativa. *See* Pomerius, Julianus
Diodorus Siculus, 30, 31
Dido, 105
Discovrse of Civill Life, A. *See* Bryskett, Lodowick
"Docter Deuyas," 26
Don Jon Gaytryge's Sermon. *See* Thoresby, John de

170

Dunbar, William, 25n
Dürer, Albrecht, 147
Dyce, Rev. Alexander, vii

E

Edward IV, of England, 153
Edwards, H. L. R., 43, 154n
Elizabeth I, Queen of England, and the cardinal virtues, 147-48, 152
Elyot, Sir Thomas, *The Boke Named the Gouernour*, "crafty conveyance" in, 32; magnificence defined in, 62; influences upon, 62n, 153; on cardinal virtues for rulers, 151; treatment of Prudence in, 151n; *Of the Knowledg which Maketh a Wise Man*, 49-50
Encheiridion Morale, 144n
Enterlude of the .iiii. Cardynal Vertues, The, 157-68
Ethicorum libri x, 61, 105-6

F

Fancy (or Fansy), allegedly Aristotelian, 47, 50; role of, in *Magnyfycence*, 47-53 passim, 89-92 passim; in medieval psychology, 50-51; mentioned, 54-55
Farnham, Willard, 127-28, 137
Ferne, John, *The Blazon of Gentrie*, 148, 152, 154-55
Fitzjames, Richard, Bishop of London, 14
Florilegii magni, 144
Florilegium morale oxoniense, 107
Folger Shakespeare Library, 77n
Formula vitae honestae. See Martin of Braga
Four cardinal virtues. See Cardinal virtues; *The Enterlude of the .iiii. Cardynal Vertues*
Four Elements, The Nature of the, 71
Fortitude, dramatized in *Magnyfycence*, 10, 69-70, 85-100, 114-26; Ciceronian *partes* of, 60, 65, 108-9, 131n, 133; Macrobian *partes* of, 65n, 108-9, 111, 131-32n, 133, 143; Andronican *partes* of, 65n; prosperity-adversity motif of, 73-85, 101-14, 143, 158-59; Fortitude, a virtue for rulers, 77-78, 82-83, 112-14, 154-55; and Temperance, 80-81; *remedium* for despair, 101-14, 121-22; cardinal virtue and gift fused, 109-11, 131-32n; and *contemptus mundi*, 131-32, 135-36, 166-67; and Horace, 141-44. See also Magnanimity, Magnificence
Fortune, in *Magnyfycence*, 3, 97, 98, 116-20 passim, 127, 128, 132, 137-39, 155, 164; and Fortitude, 61, 83, 85, 96, 135-39 passim, 165, 166
Fovre Bookes of Offices. See Barnes, Barnabe
Fox, Richard, Bishop of Winchester, 35-42 passim
France, 33-37
French, Academie, The. See La Primaudaye, Pierre de
Frost, George, viii

G

Garnesche, Sir Christopher, 25, 26. See also Skelton
Gifts of the Holy Spirit, 109-11, 131-32n
Gilbert, Allan H., 147n
Giraldus Cambrensis, equates Fortitude and magnificence, 69; cites Horace under Fortitude, 142-43; on kings and cardinal virtues, 149-50
Giustinian, Sebastian, 14-15, 43-44
Godly Queene Hester, viii, 17, 32-33n
Good Order, attributed to Skelton, viii
Gower, John, *Mirour de l'Omme*, 68
Grafton, Richard, 32
Graves, Robert, vi
Green, Peter, 77n
Greenburg, Noah, vi
Greg, W. W., vii-viii, 17
Gregory I, the Great, Pope, 79, 105

171

INDEX

Grimald, Nicholas, 84
Gringoire, Pierre, *Le Château de Labour,* 122

H

Halitgar, Bishop of Cambrai, 104
Hall, Edward, 17-18, 34
Harward, Simon, *Encheiridion Morale,* 144
Heiserman, A. R., 8, 9, 10, 25n, 46-47, 57-58
Henry V, of England, 150
Henry VII, of England, 33
Henry VIII, of England, and *Magnyfycence,* 6, 45, 95, 159; Wolsey enters service of, 33-34; relations with Howard, 38-40; and third parliament, 41-42; Skelton taught Cicero to, 77, 153; and iconography of virtues, 148; advice from Skelton, 129-31, 137, 154-55; in *.iiii. Cradynal Vertues,* 157, 159-60, 166-67
Herod, 93-94, 115
Heywood, John, v, vi, 17, 145
Higgins, John, 152
Hoby, Sir Thomas, 150n
Hoccleve, Thomas, *Regement of Prynces,* based on cardinal virtues, 82, 150; on Fortitude, 82-84, 139; on *contemptus mundi,* 139
Hogrefe, Pearl, v, 15in
Hooper, E. S., 5, 22
Horace, cited in *Magnyfycence,* 10, 87, 139-41 *passim,* 144, 155, 168; on the Golden Mean, 139-40; and Fortitude tradition, 141-44
Howard family. *See* Norfolk; Surrey, Countess of
Hrabanus Maurus, on prosperity-adversity motif of Fortitude, 79; on Fortitude *vs.* despair, 104-5, 107; on cardinal virtues for rulers, 149; mentioned, 109
Hugh of St. Victor, 110, 133
Hume, David, 39-40
Hunne, Richard, 14
Hurault, Jacques, *Politicke, Moral, and Martial Discourses,* 151-52, 154-55
Hyckescorner, 6, 25, 55, 71

I

Illvstrvm poetarvm flores, 144
"Impeachment of Wolsey, An," 16
Institvcion of a Gentleman, The, 155n
Interlude. *See* Enterlude
Isidore of Seville, 75
Ishmael, 13

J

Jacob's Well, 111n
James IV, of Scotland, 148
Jean de la Rochelle, 80
Job, 102
John of Salisbury, 110-11
Jones, H. S. V., 113
Jonson, Ben, 12
Jusserand, J. J., 63-64

K

Kalender of Shepherdes, The, 132-33, 134
Katharine of Aragon, 148
Katzenellenbogen, Adolf, 147
Kinsman, Robert S., vi, vii
Koelbing, Arthur, 5

L

Laistner, M. L. W., 103n
Lang, Joseph, *Florilegii magni,* 144
La Primaudaye, Pierre de, on parallels of "magnificence," 68-69; on prosperity-adversity motif of Fortitude, 85; on sycophants and advisers, 94; on Fortitude *vs.* despair, 112-13; based *French Academie* on Cicero, 136, 137, 153; on *contemptus mundi* and Fortitude, 136, 137; no cardinal virtues for rulers, 151; mentioned, 84, 87
Latini, Brunetto, *Li Livres dou Tresor,* 76n, 142, 143
Lay Folks' Catechism, The, 79, 80

INDEX

Legh, Gerard, *The Accedens of Armory*, 69, 152
Lehmberg, Stanford E., 151n
Liberality, in Aristotle, 46, 58-62 *passim*, 67, 73; in Thomas Aquinas, 60, 65-68 *passim*; in others, 61, 62, 68, 74, 82-84 *passim*
Lindsay, Sir David, 145
Livres dou Tresor, Li, 76n, 142, 143
Lorens, Frere, on Fortitude *vs. accidia*, 111, 118, 121; mentioned, 115, 133-34n. See also *Book of Vices and Virtues*
Louis XII, of France, 35, 36
Lovell, Sir Thomas, 41
Lydgate, John, 69
Lyly, William, 148

M
Mackie, J. D., 40n
Macrobius, cites *partes* of Fortitude, 65n, 131n, 133; on prosperity-adversity motif of Fortitude, 73, 77-78; on cardinal virtues for rulers, 77-78, 146; influence of, 78-79, 109, 111, 143, 152; mentioned, 76, 81
Magnanimity, allegedly confused with "magnificence," 62-64; equated with "magnificence," 64-69; equated with Fortitude, 69, 76, 82, 83, 152; and suicide, 102-3, 108-9, 113; complement to *contemptus mundi*, 131-32; mentioned, 10, 72-73, 85, 106, 127, 139
Magnificence, equated with Fortitude, 10, 69-70, 72-73, 94, 112, 127, 142; equated with magnanimity, 10, 64-69, 72-73, 83, 127; the Aristotelian term, 46, 47, 57-59; Skelton's source for, 57-69; relation to liberality, 58-62, 65-69 *passim*; as *remedium* for *tristitia*, 107; related to perseverance, 133
Mancinus, Dominicus, *De quatuor virtutibus*, 147n. See also Barclay, Alexander
Mankynde, despair motif in, 9, 123; extravagant dress in, 23; structure of, 71
Margaret Tudor, Queen of Scotland, 148
Marlowe, Christopher, *Dr. Faustus*, 122
Marshe, Thomas, 20
Martin of Braga, *Formula vitae honestae*, influence of, 146-47, 152, 154; on cardinal virtues for rulers, 146; Skelton's echo of, 154; mentioned, 81
Mary Magdalen, 23, 71
Mary Tudor, of France, 35
Maurus, Hrabanus. *See* Hrabanus Maurus
Maximilian I, Emperor, 147. *See also* Milan expedition
Medwall, Henry, dramatic activities of, vi, viii; *Nature*, extravagant dress in, 23; self-analysis of vices in, 24; allegorizes reason *vs.* will, 53-55; structure of, 71; despair in, 123
Michel, Dan, *Ayenbite of Inwyt*, on prosperity-adversity motif of Fortitude, 79n; on Fortitude *vs. accidia*, 111n; *contemptus mundi* in, 131-32n; modifies sub-virtues of Fortitude, 134n
Milan expedition, 35, 41-44
Milton, John, *Paradise Lost*, 49, 51-52; *Samson Agonistes*, 107, 116
Mind, Will, and Understanding. See *Wisdom*
Mirabelli, Domenico Nani. *See* Nani Mirabelli
Mirandula, Octavianus, *Illvstrvm poetarvm flores*, 144
Miro, King of Galicia, 146
Mirour de l'Omme, 68
Mirror for Magistrates, 122, 152
Mirror. *See* Mirour, Myrrour
Moloney, Michael F., 64-65
Moralium dogma philosophorum, cites Horace under Fortitude, 142, 143; influence of, 142; imparts cardinal virtues to ruler, 149-50;

173

INDEX

based on Cicero, 152-53; mentioned, 76
More, Sir Thomas, v-vi, 148
Mother Hubberd's Tale, 23
Moyle, Thomas, 18
Mundus et infans, self-anlaysis of vices in, 24; structure of, 71-72, 158; dramatizes despair, 123-24
Myrrour of Good Maners, 68, 69, 147n
Myrrour of the Chyrche, 80-81

N

Nanfan, Sir Richard, 33
Nani Mirabelli, Domenico, *Polyantheae,* 144
Nash, Ray, viii
Nashe, Thomas, 26n
Nature. See Medwall, Henry
Nature of the Four Elements, The, 71
Nelson, William, 15, 48, 77n
Nicomachean Ethics. See Aristotle
Norfolk, Thomas Howard, 2nd Duke of, and Wolsey, 14, 35-44 *passim;* foreign policy role of, 34, 35, 40-44; alleged expulsions of, 38-44 *passim;* his prodigality, 39-40; mentioned, 12
Norfolk, Thomas Howard II, 3rd Duke of, 15, 43
North, Edward, 1st Baron, 16-17
Noyons, Treaty of, 44

O

Obedience of a Christian Man, 17
"Of the Cardinall Wolse," 16

P

Patience, sub-virtue to Fortitude, 65, 106; in *Magnyfycence,* 100, 101, 107, 114-15, 118, 125; *remedium* for despair, 105-14 *passim,* 165-66; definition of in *Summa Theologica,* 106-7. See also Fortitude
Patrizi, Francesco, *De regno et regis institutione,* defines magnificence, 61; Elyot's use of, 62; on cardinal virtues of rulers, 150-51; based on Cicero, 153
Paul, Saint, 108, 119
Peckham, John, Archbishop of Canterbury, 78-80 *passim*
Peraldus, Guilielmus, *Summa de virtutibus et vitiis,* equates magnificence, magnanimity, Fortitude, 67, 76; on prosperity-adversity motif of Fortitude, 76, 81; synthesizes Cicero and Macrobius, 78; mentioned, 68-69
Perseverance, 65, 106, 132-34. See also Fortitude
Philippe, Chancellor, of Paris, 80
Phillip III, of France, 150
Play of Love, The, 17
Plotinus, 146
Politicke, Moral, and Martial Discourses, 151-52, 154-55
Pollard, A. F., 13, 16
Pollet, Maurice, vii, 13, 88, 122n
Polyantheae. See Nani Mirabelli
Pomerius, Julianus, *De vita contemplativa,* on Fortitude *vs.* despair, 102, 103; influence of, 104-5, 106, 111, 113; mentioned, 109
Practyce of Prelates, The, 17
Primaudaye, Pierre de la. See La Primaudaye
Pro Musica Antiqua, vi
Prudence, 151n. See also Cardinal virtues
Prudentius, Aurelius Clemens, 145

R

Rabanus Maurus. See Hrabanus Maurus
Ramsay, Robert L., on morality play conventions, viii-ix; on satire as purpose of *Magnyfycence,* ix, 6-7, 12-45 *passim;* on Aristotelian ideas in *Magnyfycence,* 5-6, 46-63 *passim,* 127; dismisses final stages of *Magnyfycence,* 6-7, 45; on dating of *Magnyfycence,* 20-21, 45; relies on Polydore Vergil,

41-42; assumes Skelton misread Aristotle, 58-59, 62-63, 66; on Hoccleve as Skelton's source, 82, 84; on Perseueraunce, 132-33; on Horatian allusion in *Magnyfycence*, 139-40; on *Speculum principis*, 153-54
Rastell, John, printed Skelton's drama, v, viii; *The Four Elements*, 71; prepares pageantry, 148; mentioned, vi, viii
Ratherius, Bishop of Verona, 149
Reason *vs.* will, in Skelton's non-dramatic works, 48-50; dramatized in *Magnyfycence*, 50, 51-53, 86-92 *passim*, 162-65 *passim*; in other moralities, 53-57
Reed, A. W., v
Rede Me and Be Nott Wrothe, 17, 32-33n
Redford, John, viii, 145
Regement of Prynces. See Hoccleve, Thomas
Respublica, 31-32
Ribner, Irving, 13
Rich, Edmund, *Speculum ecclesiae*, 80-81
Roo, John, 17-19
Roy, William, and Jerome Barlowe, *Rede Me and Be Nott Wrothe*, 17, 32-33n
Ruthal, Thomas, Bishop of Durham, 35, 43-44

S

Salter, F. M., 13, 154n
Saul, King, 129-30, 154
Seneca, *pseudo-*, 76. See *also* Martin of Braga
Septenaries, 109-11, 134n
Ship of Fools, The. See Barclay, Alexander
Simon of Tournai, 75n
Skelton, John, seldom viewed as dramatist, v-ix; relations with Howards, 15; brevity of his anti-Wolsey periods, 19-22; flyting of, 25, 26; views on reason *vs.* will,

30-31, 48-53 *passim;* familiar with *De inventio*, 60n; admired Macrobius, 77-78; relations with Robert Whittinton, 77; taught Cicero to Henry VIII, 77, 153; advised Henry VIII, 129-31, 137, 154-55
—WORKS
Achademios, vii
"Against the Scottes," 15
"Against Venemous Tongues," 30n, 39n
"Agaynste a Comely Coystrowne," 25, 26, 30n
Bibliotheca Historica (trans.), 30-31
The Bowge of Court, 13, 36, 88
"Chorus de Dis contra Scottos," 15
Colin Clout, 20, 21, 23, 26, 27, 63
Garlande of Laurell, vii, 3, 15, 20, 21, 77-78
Garnesche poems, 25, 26, 30n, 60n
Howe the Douty Duke of Albany, 20, 26
Magnyfycence (selected items only), modern productions of, vi; modern interpretations of, 3-9; psychological allegory in, 50-53, 86-92 *passim*, 162-65 *passim;* meaning of "magnificence" in, 59-62 *passim*, 64-67 *passim*, 69-70; analogies with Hoccleve's *Regement*, 83-84; analysis of first conflict, 85-95; Horatian allusion in, 87, 139-44 *passim;* sycophancy in, 88-94 *passim;* analysis of second conflict, 95-100; dramatizes despair motif, 114-21, 122-23n; *contemptus mundi* in, 124-25, 127-39 *passim;* relationship to *Speculum principis*, 129-31, 153-54; analogies with *.iiii. Cardynal Vertues*, 157-67
The Nigramansir, vii, viii, 13
"Of the Death of . . . Edwarde the Forth," 129

175

"Paiauntis . . . played in Ioyows Garde," vii
Replycacion Agaynst Certayne Yong Scolers . . . , A, 19-20, 60n
Speculum principis, Wolsey and Ishmael allusion, 13; *contemptus mundi* in, 129-31, 137; draws on prosperity-adversity concept, 153-54
Speke, Parrot, 20-29 *passim*, 48-49
"Upon the . . . Dethe of . . . Northumberlande," 30, 48
"Vertu . . . the souerayne enterlude," vii
"Ware the Hauke," 30n
Why Come Ye Nat to Court?, 20, 21, 23, 29n, 31, 48. See also *Godly Queene Hester; Good Order*
Smaragdus of St. Michel, 149
Somme le Roi. See Lorens, Frere
Somnium scipionis. See Macrobius
Speculum doctrinale. See Vincent of Beauvais
Speculum ecclesiae, 80-81
Spenser, Edmund, magnificence-magnanimity in *Faerie Queene,* 63-64, 67; cardinal virtues in *Faerie Queene,* 64, 67, 150; despair in *Faerie Queene,* 113, 116, 122, 124; mentioned, 12, 23
Suelzer, Sister Mary Josephine, 103n
Suffolk, Charles Brandon, 1st Duke of, 41
Suicide, 130. See also Despair
Summa Theologica. See Thomas Aquinas, Saint
Surrey, Countess of, 15
Surrey, Earl of. See Norfolk

T

Thomas Aquinas, Saint, modifies Cicero's virtues, 59-60, 65-67, 106; on magnificence-liberality, 59-61; on magnificence-magnanimity, 64-67; subsumes Macrobian to Ciceronian *partes* of Fortitude, 65n, 131n, 133; on Fortitude and patience *vs.* despair, 106-7, 113; mentioned, 61, 69, 78, 105, 119
Thomas of Sutton, 67
Thoresby, John de, *The Lay Folks' Catechism,* 79, 80
Tournai, 35, 41, 75n
Treatyse of a Galaunt, A, 37n
Tristitia, opposed by Fortitude and patience, 105-14 *passim;* in *Magnyfycence,* 116-21 *passim.* See *also* Despair
Tyndale, William, 17, 32

U

Ubi sunt, 116-17

V

Venetian ambassador. See Giustinian, Sebastian
Vergil, Polydore, *Anglica Historia,* 33-37 *passim,* 41-43
Vincent of Beauvais, *Speculum doctrinale,* equates magnificence and magnanimity, 67; on prosperity-adversity motif of Fortitude, 76, 143; cites Horace under Fortitude, 143; Skelton's acquaintance with, 143-44; mentioned, 78
Virgil (Publius Vergilius Maro), vi
Virtues. See Cardinal virtues
Voyage of the Wandering Knight, The, 112, 154-55

W

Wanhope. See Despair
Ward, A. W., 4, 8
Warham, William Archbishop of Canterbury, 35, 41-42
Warren, Leslie C., 151n
Warton, Thomas, vii, 13
Whittinton, Robert, glosses prosperity-adversity in Cicero, 76, 84; relation to Skelton, 77; translation of *De officiis* cited, 88, 96, 135; translated *Formula vitae honestae,* 146-47n

INDEX

Will. *See* Reason *vs.* will
Wisdom, Who Is Christ, satire in, 6; allegorizes reason *vs.* will, 56-57; structure of, 71; despair in, 123
Wolsey, Thomas, allegedly satirized as Magnyfycence, 5, 22; allegedly satirized as vices in *Magnyfycence,* 6, 22-32; allegedly satirized in Skelton's early work, 13; legatine powers of, 13-15; satirized only in 1520's, 15-22; Skelton's dedications to, 19-20, 26; alleged "prophecies" about, 27-28; Calais residence of, 33, 36-37; French policy of, 34-36; and Milan expedition, 35, 43-44; advanced by Fox, 37; and Howard's expulsion, 38-39; mentioned, 3, 7, 10, 12, 13, 15, 45, 46, 70
Workes of Armorie, 152

Y

Yonge, James, *The Gouernaunce of Prynces,* 150

www.ingramcontent.com/pod-product-compliance
Lightning Source LLC
Chambersburg PA
CBHW030112010526
44116CB00005B/217